PERSONAL POWER

PERSONAL POWER

The Guide To Power For Today's Working Woman

**Arleen
LaBella**

**Dolores
Leach**

CareerTrack Publications

89 88 87 86 85   14 13 12 11 10 9 8 7

To our mothers
Elda M. LaBella and Margaret M. Leach
who, through their love and confidence,
have empowered us.

Contents

We first and foremost want to express our appreciation to the thousands of participants in our workshops who have shared the problems, joys and challenges of being working women with us. Their experience and feedback offers much of the foundation of this book.

Next we want to thank those women who have fostered understanding by bringing women's issues to the forefront of the American conscience. They are our role models and their work is our inspiration. Specifically, Sandra Bem, Patricia Bidol, Barbara Bunker, Betty Friedan, Selma Greenberg, Betty Lehan Harrigan, Margaret Henning, Ann Jardim, Rosabeth Moss Kanter, Natasha Josefowitz, Margaret James-Neil, Alice Sargent, Anne Wilson Schaef, and Edith Seashore.

We appreciate our colleagues Laura Buglione, Irene Burke Carew, Ellen Goodstein, Rich Goodstein, Valari Jack, Peggy Lichter, Elizabeth Loughran, Grace Morlock, Dennis O'Brien and Patricia Leach Tessier for their helpful suggestions on content. To our editors, Martha Henderson, Judy Johnston and Jeff Salzman for not only editing but understanding our message, and to Robert Taylor for his work on graphic design, many thanks. For their ability to read our handwriting and turn it into a typewritten page, thanks to Grace Morlock, Laurie Watkins, Alicia Quillen, Ronnie Moore and Susan Sprouse. We are grateful to Jimmy Calano and Jeff Salzman, our publishers, for their encouragement and confidence in us from the very beginning. Arleen gives special thanks to Mary McCreary and Stephanie Marks for the loving care they have given her son so she could spend guilt-free time writing this book. We value the love, support and constant stimulation given us by our sisters, brothers, parents, husbands and children. Lastly we thank each other for her patience, sense of humor and continual encouragement.

Introduction

Women were brought up to support power, not exercise it. No matter how far we've come in the last two decades, that one blunt fact still creates nagging problems for most professional women.

Which is not to say we haven't come a long way. In our own lifetimes we have seen a gradual loosening of the sex-role stereotypes that for so long have limited both men and women. Today women are moving into executive positions where we are required to exercise authority and power. In all areas of work we are recognizing the need to make our competencies visible, take more risks, and compete in previously unacceptable ways. Likewise, more and more men are voicing their dissatisfaction with the limited rewards of the traditional breadwinner's role. They are faced with the challenge of developing and expressing the more nurturing and adaptive parts of their personalities. In the personal realm, both men and women are challenged by the new forms our relationships are taking and the new family structures that are emerging. Clearly, this is a time of transition — very exciting, but equally confusing.

One of the fundamental obstacles women continue to face in gaining positions of power is the organization itself. The sad truth is that for the most part the American power structure is still stacked against us. Let there be no doubt: Organizations are cultures which govern behavior, and as such their impact on individual success or failure is great. The power structures of today's organizations commonly present numerous obstacles to the advancement of people who do not fully understand their complex workings. Typically, these people are women, who have had less access to experiences which can teach them the ins and outs of the system.

Although it is unrealistic to think that equality will come quickly, there is much that women can do to accelerate the process. Our success as women in the American work culture depends on our ability to understand the system in which we work and to develop the flexibility to respond and initiate within that system. For many of us, this requires adapting and becoming comfortable with new behaviors.

Many of these behaviors are linked with a sense of being powerful. Though feminism has made great strides in establishing the legitimacy of women's presence in political, social and economic power arenas, the subject of women and power can still elicit dramatic reactions. Most of us were not brought up to think of ourselves as powerful or "in control," and the rest of adult society was not taught to accept us as such. Consequently, as women move into roles where we are expected to be in control and to act on our authority, we often experience feelings of awkwardness, which are shared by the people around us.

As our feelings of entitlement grow, so do our desires to share and exercise power. The first step in the empowering process is the simple acknowledgement that power can be positive. Power is the ability to get things done, to mobilize our internal and external resources in the pursuit of a goal, and to influence those around us.

A great many of us, however, carry negative images of power, and therefore deny the fullfilment of our potentials. For example, women often link power with selfishness. Many women believe that being powerful means dominating or taking advantage of other people. No doubt all of us have at some time witnessed such behaviors in powerful people we have known. For those of us who have typically been socialized to think of ourselves as self-sacrificing helpmates, the desire to deny a selfish image is very strong. Of course, many of us are powerful people — but often choose to recognize ourselves as such only when we are in nurturing, helping or supportive roles.

Women sometimes reject the concept of power because we connect it with destructiveness. We fear that being powerful will destroy the stable and loving relationships we have worked hard to develop. And, in fact, many women do report that they are confronted with hostility and rejection when they attempt to exercise power. With so much at stake, many times we decide that the price is too high; we would rather feel powerless than rejected.

The challenge is to reframe the concept of power, and look at it in terms that emphasize its positive aspects. To do this it is necessary to separate power into its two major components: *personal power* and *position power*. Personal power is the power that is gained from a person's internal capacities and qualities — acquired as a result of behavior, attitudes and wisdom. Position power, on the other hand, is power that is granted as a function of the *role* a person plays. For example, people in executive roles have legitimate power by virtue of their rank, regardless of their personal qualities and capacities (although their personal power certainly had something to do with getting the position power).

Personal power is not new to most women. Using it to gain position power is. In general, it has been men in our society who have acquired position power, while women have been taught to develop personal qualities to become powerful in much less overt ways. Most women have learned to achieve goals through inter-personal skills such as persuasion and conciliation while keeping at the sidelines, safely away from "the action." Women striving for success place a high value on job skills — often more than men do — with the hope that if we perform well we will be noticed, rewarded and promoted. Unfortunately, it doesn't always work that way. Women who seek position power in the work place need an extra edge. We must project our capacities, values, emotion and intellect through a style of self-projection that *creates* personal power. Personal power emerges from con-

Dimensions of Personal Power

Powerless	Powerful	Empowering	Overpowering
Out of control	In control	Delegates and shares control	Dominates
Uninformed	Informed	Informing	Withholds information
Helpless	Self-reliant	Helpful	Takes over or offers no help at all
Insecure	Confident and secure	Compliments and reinforces others' strengths	Arrogant
Inadequate	Capable	Trusts others' capabilities	Pushy, conceited
Fearful	Risk-taker	Offers others challenging opportunities and supports their efforts	Reckless, self-absorbed

scientiously developed behaviors which are often subtle and reflect a sophisticated understanding of the organization, people and situations we work with.

The purpose of this book is to help you understand and cultivate those personal qualities that will enable you to play more powerful roles, and gain greater comfort and satisfaction in those roles. That certainly does not mean that women should strive to become "just like men" in order to succeed. On the contrary, the life-supporting characteristics associated with traditional female roles are desperately needed in the American work place, not only to improve the quality of work life, but also to increase productivity.

The concept of personal power is further defined and illuminated in chapter one. Chapter two provides a framework for understanding the traditional sex-role expectations that present obstacles to women's acquisition of power in the workplace. The remaining chapters transform these qualities into the ability to handle critical situations.

Before you begin chapter one, allow us as authors to step out of the narrative for a moment to make a couple of personal comments about what we've written. First of all, when we talk about the organizational barriers that are set up for women, we do not mean to limit these barriers to women. Men of minority groups also experience many of the same problems. Further, we recognize that for non-white women, whose racial differences are added to gender differences, the problems become much more complex. Nevertheless, we believe that the majority of issues addressed in this book transcend many cultural differences and apply in some way to all people who traditionally have been denied access to power structures.

Secondly, when we talk about the differences between groups of people (male and female, for instance) we do not presume to speak for all people and all circumstances. What determines membership in the traditional "white male system" versus a more liberated system is not one's sex or race, but one's values. People don't fit neatly into categories. Many women live according to the values of the traditional white male system and some men live according to the values of a more liberated system.

As two aspiring professional women ourselves, we share many experiences, concerns and hopes with other women. Therefore we have prefaced chapters two through nine with excerpts from our own lives. We believe that through such sharing of common experiences, women will more easily learn to identify and trust their inner sources of strength. Ultimately, it will be that strength which will enable us to break through the internal and external barriers to a full and natural expression of ourselves as powerful people.

Arleen LaBella
Dolores Leach

May, 1983

PERSONAL
POWER

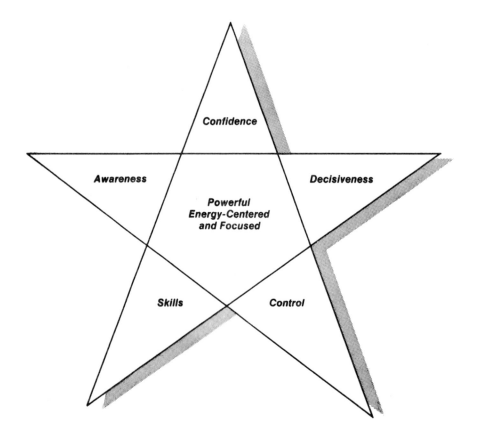

1. Personal Power

Personal power is a tough concept to pin down. We all recognize power when we see it exercised: the president of the United States making cabinet appointments, an executive launching a new project, a mother convincing her child to attempt a new task. But how is it that we know a person has power even before we see him or her exercise it? What are the personal, human qualities that make up power? And, most important, how can we develop these qualities in ourselves?

Simply put, personal power is the process of balancing and directing your creative energy. There are five key elements in this process: *confidence, decisiveness, control, skills* and *awareness*. To help illustrate how these elements work together we have developed a model called *the power star*. Each point on the star stands for one of the components of personal power. The center of the star is the source of the creative energy by which you nourish, motivate and renew yourself — you might consider it to be your "center" as well. A woman in one of our workshops described it as the "home base" she carries with her at all times.

These five elements strike a perfect balance in the star. They must also exist in balance in the personally powerful individual. Let's take a closer look at how you can develop and balance them in your life.

Confidence

Because of its significance for the personally powerful individual, we give confidence top position on the star. Confidence is the means by which you present yourself to the world, the continuous communication of the powerful you. But how can that process be communicated when so often confidence is the last thing you feel?

No one has a window to your soul. People don't know how you are feeling unless you give signals that tell them how you are feeling — or, even more important in a professional environment, how you *want* them to think you are feeling. Projecting confidence is largely a result of being in charge of the signals you send.

You put out and pick up signals all the time, whether or not you are aware of it. Say you go into an office supply store and the salesperson greets you with a mumbled hello while looking down at the floor and fidgeting with a pencil. Is she confident? Of course not. She's obviously having a low-self-image day; you want to excuse yourself to find another salesperson (or you end up buying more than you need just to make her feel better). On the other hand, if she greets you with a smile, direct eye contact and a straight, relaxed posture, your impression is entirely different. You are comfortable and confident knowing she is comfortable and confident.

The signals of insecurity are obvious to everyone. Lip biting, foot shuffling and fidgeting are all parts of the nonverbal behavior that communicates insecurity. *Nonverbal* is the key: The expression of confidence or insecurity is largely a phenomenon of silent language. Our unconscious facial expressions, gestures and movements express our feelings far more eloquently than our most carefully chosen words — they can also undermine our most carefully chosen words.

Surely you have had an experience with a friend or coworker that left you anxious, upset or angry, yet when you reviewed what was said you couldn't find any reason why you should be so bothered. But how about the nonverbal aspects of the interaction? Think again: wasn't there an ever-so-subtle lift of an eyebrow, a slight turning away (the infamous "cold shoulder") or a quiet sigh of exasperation as you talked? Any of these could communicate far more than what was actually said. The trick is to look and listen beyond the verbal message to the nonverbal message which colors it.

Consider the following components of nonverbal communication and how they contribute to powerful, powerless and overpowering behavior in you and the people in your life.

Eye Contact

Using direct eye contact is not only a way to send a powerful message, it is also a tool for assessing the effect of your message on another person. Say you are going into your boss's office to request a raise. (Naturally, you have already paid attention to his or her nonverbal behaviors to see if he or she is receptive. If you had observed a bad mood or high-pressure day, you would have strategically set up an appointment where you could be assured of his or her full attention). When the moment comes to make the request it is critical that you look your boss straight in the eye. After all, you can't expect him or her to take you seriously (at least not *as* seriously) if you are gazing at the ceiling or the floor while you talk.

This goes for setting limits with someone, saying no and standing up to a conflict. If something is worth saying, it is worth saying directly, with confident, self-assured eye contact. It makes all the difference in the world.

Posture

Have you ever been surprised to find out that a person is much shorter than you thought? One of our workshop participants described a nurse in her organization as the "tallest little person" she had ever known. She was responding, not to the woman's size, but to the presence and image projected through her erect, energized posture. Another woman described a relatively short bank president by saying "he looks like his feet are planted on the ground while he is reaching for the sky." For both the nurse and the bank president, posture was an effective means of expressing self-confidence and, ultimately, personal power.

Your image is often first communicated by the way you carry yourself and move through space. Your walk (your posture on the move) lets others know whether you are to be noticed, respected, feared or ignored. Look at your posture and analyze what message you are communicating. An exercise that will help you understand the power of posture is called "What's Your Bumper Sticker?" Here's how it works: the next time you are with a group of friends or coworkers try to sum up in a few words what message each person is communicating through body language. For example, a woman who is fairly erect, but has slightly slouched shoulders and a forward tilt to her head, could give the impression of being a little under the weight of things. Her bumper sticker might be "Overloaded." Try it; you'll be amazed at how simple body position can deliver such a clear and complete message.

This exercise will also increase your awareness of how others perceive you. The fact is, what we think we are communicating and what we are actually communicating are often two very different things, simply because so much of our posture is habitual. The point of assessing your own body message is to make yourself aware and in charge of what you're communicating, so you can communicate confidence in every appropriate situation.

When you use your body language to communicate confidence, you begin to actually *feel* confident. This is one of the truly exciting benefits of taking charge of your behavior — you begin to take charge of your feelings as well.

	Powerful	Powerless	Overpowering
Eye Contact	direct; eyes talk and listen	avoiding direct eye contact	staring, glaring, looking "down" on
Facial Expression	congruent with your verbal message	incongruent (i.e. smiling while angry)	lifted eyebrow, pursed lips, squinting
Posture	erect, energized	slouched, no energy, immobile	rigid, "puffed up" chest
Voice	clear, even paced, well projected	too slow, too low, stammering, pitch goes up at end of sentence	loud, demanding, too fast to be understood
Body Movement/ Gestures	minimal, deliberate, used to add emphasis to verbal message	too many gestures, fidgeting, hands touching face, hair, mouth	pointing finger, broad gestures and movement that violate others' personal space

Body Movements and Gestures

The one important question to ask yourself when assessing your own body movements and gestures is, "do they add to or detract from my message?"

Hand gestures are generally thought to complement conversation if they do not distract the other person's eye contact from your own. A good rule of thumb (no pun intended) is to keep your hands below your neckline. This means no fingers, pencils or paper clips in your mouth, no hair twirling and no playing with your earrings.

An office manager in an organization where we once consulted mentioned that she felt her input about a new marketing approach was unjustly ignored. This upset her, because she believed her new strategy would really increase the company's sales. The woman seemed to have a lot of self-confidence, so we wondered what the problem could be. At the next staff meeting, which we sat in on, we saw the problem clearly: Whenever the woman made a comment or presented an idea she automatically covered her mouth with her hand. No wonder she wasn't taken seriously! Her verbal message was right on target, but her nonverbal message communicated "I'm not really sure; don't take me too seriously." This depowering mannerism was so obvious that we were amazed she was unaware of it. When we told her about it she was surprised, and ultimately relieved. The last time we talked to her she said that by eliminating this one simple gesture she felt she was beginning to be received more respectfully by her fellow workers.

Other power-robbing behaviors common to women include: cocking the head to one side during conversation, swaying back and forth on one hip, smiling too frequently, crossing the legs when standing and touching any part of the body. All of these communicate insecurity and powerlessness (interesting that these are some of the behaviors most encouraged when we were growing up).

Breath and Voice

More and more frequently, doctors and psychologists are telling us about the significant role breathing plays in managing stress, building physical strength and putting us in touch with our "centers." We don't often think of breath as a source of energy, but it is. And at those times when we need an extra jolt of confidence, it is critical. For example, effective breathing is as essential for handling a tough situation on the job as it is for running the Boston marathon. The next time you feel called upon to give a little extra, and particularly when you face a tight spot where your confidence is put to the test, make a conscious effort to breath fully and deeply. The effect is empowering.

Breath is also essential to voice quality, which is essential to the ability to project confidence. A manager once approached us during a public seminar and said that because of his high-pitched voice he was too self-conscious to ask a question during the workshop. His supervisor had told him his voice made him less effective in his job (he worked for a large industrial firm) and would probably stand in the way of future promotions. As he talked we noticed that he cut off his breath at his throat, thereby giving his voice a gravelly, squeaky quality. We told him he was not exercising the full use of his voice potential, and gave him instructions to breathe fully into his chest, abdomen and legs to bring energy and strength to his entire body. After a few simple exercises, he could hear his voice changing quality and tone. What he had thought was an irreversible curse was merely a result of not breathing deeply enough. Once he had mastered proper breathing, he was able to produce a strong, resonant, firm speaking voice that added a lot to his projection of confidence — and to his self-confidence as well.

Two Rules of Confidence

The first one is simple: practice, practice, practice. The skills of projecting confidence through body language, like all skills, can be learned and mastered. But only if you practice. Practice by yourself in front a mirror; practice by trying new techniques on the people you deal with every day. Soon you'll know what works for you and what doesn't, and the productive behaviors will become a natural part of your communication style.

The second rule is *fake it till you make it.*

Obviously, it's a bit tongue-in-cheek. No one is seriously suggesting that we should bluff our way through life. But at those times when our skill and competence are overshadowed by our nervousness and anxiety, we need to adopt the power behaviors that reinforce our *confidence,* so that our *competence* has a chance to shine through.

Case in point: Jill was an administrative assistant in a large retail company. She knew the product lines inside out, wanted desperately to move out of staff into sales, and was confident she could do the job — except for one thing: the thought of making a sales presentation turned her knees into jello. Jill tried to overcome her fear by attending one of our assertiveness seminars. At noon she approached us looking very depressed. She would never be able to do it, she said. After listening to us all morning, she was sure that there are some people who are "naturals" at public speaking, and the rest of the world would just have to be satisfied sitting on the sidelines. Naturally we were flattered, but we were also a bit annoyed. By labeling us "naturals," Jill was discounting all the hard work we had put into developing our speaking skills. She was not around ten years ago, when one of us was so anxious she used to get sick before giving a class at the local YMCA. Nor was she around the time the other of us lost her train of thought so badly during a talk that she had to apologize to the group and begin all over.

More important than this, though, was that Jill just assumed that no amount of practice could get her to be a competent, persuasive salesperson. Her attitude illustrates a problem that many professionals of both sexes have: "How can I compete with people better than me?" Of course there will always be some people who are better at something than we are — whether because of more experience, stronger resources and, yes, even more innate ability. But so what? We're not in competition with all the other people in the world; we don't need to measure ourselves against anyone else's yardstick; we don't have to prove anything to anyone else. Our only goal is to personally empower ourselves by believing that if we go after what we want, we will get better and better through practice — to the point where we can use our full potential to achieve our own goals, our own way, on our own schedule.

Fortunately, Jill decided not to give up. Instead, she started sitting in on any and all of the sales presentations she could. She observed successful people in her organization, and used them as role models. At night she went home and gave the sales presentations to herself in the bathroom mirror . . . then to a friend . . . then to one of the saleswomen she had befriended and who served as a mentor. In her practice, Jill used a wonderful technique advocated by Timothy Gallwey in his book *The Inner Game of Tennis*. Gallwey tells readers to *program* themselves for what they want (a more powerful serve, for example) and then watch the motion of someone who has already achieved the goal. Don't overanalyze, he says; simply absorb what you see by trying to feel what the other person feels. Then take some time to picture yourself hitting the ball in the same way, imagining as much visual and tactile detail as possible. Jill applied this visualization technique to public speaking, and found it very helpful.

After much visual and actual rehearsal, Jill approached her boss to tell him she wanted a crack at a sales job. Her boss agreed to give her an interview in front of a group of veteran salespeople.

No matter how many times Jill had given the sales presentation in practice and faithfully imagined her success, on the day of her interview her knees turned right back into jello. This is where the second rule, "fake it till you make it," came in handy for Jill. In spite of her anxiety, she deliberately and consciously adopted all the techniques and mannerisms of confidence: She took a couple of full, deep breaths before entering the room;

walked in purposefully; stood erect (despite the visible shaking of her knees); used her breath to give depth and resonance to her voice; and managed her gestures and facial expressions to highlight what she was saying — just the way she had practiced. As she got further into the material, she began to feel a lot more comfortable. Happily, she noticed her audience became a lot more comfortable too, and seemed to listen with interest and enjoyment.

When she had finished the presentation, even before she received group feedback, she knew she had done a good job. Her practice and attitude adjustment techniques had paid off for her the very first time she used them. A week later she left the support staff for good, entering the sales training program which has led to her desired career.

Decisiveness

To be a professional is to make decisions. And the better you learn to make decisions, the faster you will advance. That's why decisiveness receives the second point on the personal power star.

Decisiveness is made up of three basic elements: 1) the ability to analyze the costs and benefits of each option, 2) the freedom to allow ourselves the right to make a mistake, and 3) the freedom to allow ourselves the right to not be liked. Difficulty with any of these prerequisites can be a stumbling block to effective decision-making, and many women have difficulty with all three. Let's look at each more closely to find out why this is so and what we can do about it.

Analyze Costs and Benefits

The most important element of skillful decision-making is the ability to fully *appreciate the costs and benefits contingent upon each possible decision*. Usually, in analyzing the various options, we come up with one that we think will bring us the greatest gain. But in this process we also come to realize that we must give up one or more options. Here is where many women run into difficulty. Unlike our male counterparts, women are generally socialized to concentrate on the *process* of events rather than the end result. And we often resist making changes when the process appears too difficult. In other words, we tend to focus on — and get stuck at — the "how" phase, rather than the outcome, or "what" stage. We look at the costs of implementing decisions rather than the benefits.

One of our former seminar students illustrates this process beautifully. Jane, a telephone operator recently divorced and now living with her three sons, laments the fact that she did not pursue a college degree while she was married, as her ex-husband Frank did. She based her decision (as have millions of women like her) on the criterion that managing a home and caring for children and an ambitious husband left no time for studies. (She was acutely aware of the costs!) Her husband, on the other hand, was determined to obtain the college degree necessary to advance his career. (He was acutely aware of the benefits!) Never once did Jane imagine herself with a college degree in hand, or consider what it would do for her. She was able to visualize only the process, not the result.

Many issues complicate such situations. There's the traditional expectation that the man's career is more important than the woman's. In our society the man has typically been the one to "go to work" while the woman stayed behind to "keep house." Had Jane and Frank allowed themselves to think past these conventional notions, they could have negotiated a more equal sharing of child care, home maintenance and other tasks, while both pursued a college degree — and ultimately reaped the rewards. But their socialization fixed them on the costs of Jane's education, clouding the prospect of future benefits and crippling their ability to think through the decision in any other way.

The Right to Make Mistakes

Now let's move to the second element of decisiveness: *allowing ourselves the right to make mistakes*. The natural inclination is to hold off on making a decision until we have all the information we need. But that can be (and often is) carried too far. If we wait until we are 100 percent sure that we are making the Right rather than the Wrong decision, we can be 100 percent sure of only one thing — we will never make any decision at all. To be decisive and proactive, we often need to act *long before* we're convinced we're doing the right thing. Effective managers are labeled effective, not necessarily because of the number of correct decisions they make, but because they can make decisions, period. Think for a minute; do you see many wishy-washy people in positions of power? Of course not! And if you do see one, you can be sure he or she was put there by someone more powerful who needs a yes-person.

Waiting to be sure is a never-ending process. In the professional world it is considered dependent, passive and powerless behavior, which communicates that you are waiting for reassurance from a stronger, more independent source. In the long run it leaves you vulnerable to other peoples' decisions; you end up living for their goals instead of your own.

Fear generally lies behind indecisiveness: fear of making a mistake, fear of punishment, fear of failure, and fear of criticism. No wonder so many of us get stuck here; after all, each of these fears are real possibilities. But you must not allow them to immobilize you. The next time these fears are hindering your decision-making, ask yourself, "what actually will happen if I fail?" The truth is, you may be better equipped to deal with the consequences of a wrong decision than you think.

To conquer your fear there are three ideas you should repeat over and over in your mind as you gear up for your next big decision. The first is *I'm not the only one who's ever made a mistake.* It can be very comforting to remember that everyone has made mistakes and millions are doing it right along with you.

The second idea is *I'll live* (otherwise known as "this too shall pass"). Think about it: When was the last time you were absolutely confident of a decision, and it blew up in your face?

You not only lived through the bad results of the decision, but also through the criticism and the agony of 20-20 hindsight.

The third idea, and perhaps the most valuable, is *I've learned a good lesson.* Turn lemons into lemonade! Life is a process of trial and error, and each time you make a mistake there's great comfort in knowing you have just learned a lesson that — if you're smart — you will never repeat again.

And as with most everything else we've talked about, practice makes perfect. The more you experience yourself as being decisive and living with the consequences, both positive and negative, the easier the decision-making process becomes. Through practice, you gain perspective on your decisions and realize that only by risking failure can you free yourself to make the choices that will bring you a fuller, richer and more creative life.

The Right to Not Be Liked

The third element of decisiveness is *allowing yourself the right to not be liked.* Have you ever had to make a decision to fire someone, cut a budget, offer unwelcome criticism or refuse a request? The consequences of such decisions can make you an unpopular member of the team, at least temporarily. What happens if you decide to take the safe road? You won't be challenged or called upon to take risks, but taking the course of least resistance leads to lack of recognition, fewer promotions and, in the long run, little satisfaction. If you have any interest at all in moving into a position of power, whether in your professional life or your home life, it is absolutely necessary to manage the feeling of being unliked, unpopular and left out.

Pattie, a coworker of ours, was having some difficulty with her teen-age son. She had set a limit with him on the amount of time he could spend with his friends, and he decided to not speak to her for a week! When we asked Pattie how she managed, she said she understood his need to be angry and punishing, and she would patiently wait for him to come around. She knew his strategy was to manipulate her into changing her mind; she also knew that as long as she stuck with her decision (which she still thought was the right one), she would have to deal with the consequences of his anger.

It helps, in situations like these, to have our support systems clear. If Pattie had felt insecure she might have been tempted to give in. But her husband was solidly behind her, and with his support she was able to remain powerful because the approval of her son became less important. The same holds true in work situations. If we have a strong personal and professional support system, we do not need the constant approval of the people we manage. One newly appointed manager accurately summed up this dynamic by saying, "I'm finally ready to trade being liked for being respected."

Control

Next on the personal power star is control. Control can be divided into two basic categories: *self-control,* the control we have with ourselves, and *influence*, the control we have with others.

Let's look at self-control first. The importance of self-control can be seen as the expression of the basic human needs for freedom and self-direction. There is nothing more infuriating than the feeling that we are being manipulated against our will by outside forces, and nothing more frightening than the feeling that we have lost control internally.

It seems that in our stressful society, we need more and more to have the sense that we are in control of ourselves. This is evident in America's growing commitment to health and physical discipline. David McClelland, a major researcher and author in power motivation, points out that people, and particularly women, associate power with being in control of their bodies. Wonderful! What better way to express and use power in all aspects of our lives than through physical fitness?

If you aren't already a part of the fitness movement, we suggest you start. Our culture is full of information for people in every situation and with every interest, from diet, nutrition and exercise to yoga, biofeedback and rolfing — all designed to reinforce our ability to feel in control of our own bodies, and in control (rather than under the control) of our environments. Best of all, self-control is just one benefit of physical development. The health and longevity benefits are also enormous, not to mention the emotional benefits of living a more vital, less stressful life. The message here is clear: use your physical resources to support your psychological resources.

Another aspect of self-control for the personally powerful person is the control over what we express, when and to whom. This, however, does not mean the freedom to express exactly what we are experiencing at the exact moment we are experiencing it. The key is *self*-control; the ability to limit your self-expression to that which is appropriate to the person, time and place.

For instance, Lynne, a manager at a major airline, got angry with her boss when he passed on inaccurate information at a department manager's meeting. She got even angrier when, after she challenged him, he denied it — making her appear foolish in front of everyone at the meeting.

Lynne knew she was right and reasoned that she would be doing a service to her coworkers by bringing up her boss's error during the meeting. Good idea, bad timing. Pointing out the mistake in front of everyone was clearly embarrassing to her boss, and probably seemed like a grandstand play to everyone else. Because she was angered by the misinformation given by her boss, she probably communicated her anger nonverbally, coming across as belligerent rather than reasonable. This explains her boss's defensive response. What Lynne should have done was use the option to confront her boss when they were alone. That way she would have the opportunity to clarify the intention of her message, and he would have saved face. She could have then given her coworkers the correct information in a follow-up memo. This approach would be less efficient time-wise, perhaps, but far superior in human relations.

Which is not to say we should put a lid on our feelings. The best strategy is to allow our feelings to surface internally, then weigh the short- and long-range costs and benefits of expressing ourselves. Sometimes it is best to speak up right away (for instance, if Lynne's boss's wrong information would have invalidated a number of decisions yet to be made at the meeting). But generally, waiting is worth it. If the issue is important enough to go to the mat over, the feelings won't dissipate with time; they will only be clarified and more fully expressed — and you will be in control of the circumstances, timing and yourself.

Controlling what we express also means controlling what we express to ourselves. We all have a "little voice" in our heads, a continuous mental dialogue through which we interpret the events of the moment. What that voice says is essential to our personal power, and indeed to our functioning as human beings.

Imagine that you had an unresolved fight in the morning with a loved one. More than likely, you go to work with a thundercloud hanging over your head. All day you are less flexible than usual in dealing with the difficulties that arise on the job. Maybe you make an otherwise minor incident such as a late delivery or problem with an uncooperative staff member explode totally out of proportion. As a result you leave work even more anxious and upset at the end of the day. The chain reaction continues that evening at home, and the next thing you know you are well on your way down the negative spiral. Your world changes. You become self-critical and self-deprecating. You respond to the people around you as "enemies," and even worse, you unleash your greatest enemy of all — that person inside of all of us who makes statements like "I'm stupid," "I'm depressed," I can't handle the pressures at work," "I can't get along with so and so," "I'm incompetent," "I'm selfish" and on and on, until every insecurity you've experienced in the last fifteen years is clearly focused in your mind.

This is a familiar pattern for most people who deal with the challenges and pressures of a full personal and professional life. Does the pattern sound familiar to you? If so, what do you do about it? If you're like most people, usually nothing productive. At the risk of sounding like your mother for a minute, we would like to give you a little six-word lecture: *Stop it! You're wasting your time.*

But how? The answer is so simple — we've experienced it and know it works! Consciously interrupt yourself and redirect the critical negative energy into positive, nourishing self-affirmation.

Easier said than done? Of course. But consider: have you ever been very involved in a certain activity, and a crying child runs in with his or her knee badly skinned? Your immediate reaction is to put aside your work and tend to the child. The process of turning self-critical statements into self-affirming ones is similar. We must give the crying child inside of ourselves the same top-priority attention.

How to Do it

Think of your brain as the computer terminal of your body, and you the programmer. If you program yourself to think "I'm no good" then sure enough, your computer will output feelings of worthlessness. Not only that, it will motivate you to prove it is right, and you will seek out situations that validate your worthlessness.

On the other hand, if your program is "I have strengths, I am valuable," you will expect to be treated with care and respect, and seek to validate your expectations in everything you do.

A good way to stop the journey down the negative spiral is to outline specifically what you value in yourself. The list could take the form of what you do well, what you enjoy or specific behaviors you do that please you. In writing this list you are developing your self-affirming computer program to intervene the next time your overly-critical self emerges. As a practical exercise, try listing on paper ten specific behaviors that you enjoy, do well or value. From these choose one overall statement as the basis for your self-validation statement.

This too may be easier said than done. Recently a workshop participant said she could find no statement that could help validate and capture the powerful person inside her. We asked her to recall a time when she felt happy, confident and pleased with herself. She struggled to think but finally gave up, explaining that she was usually pretty self-critical. So we asked if there was a time when she at least didn't give herself a hard time. At this she smiled and said that she had changed a flat tire on the way home from work the week before.

"What did you think to yourself after you fixed the flat?" we asked.

Her answer: "I can take care of myself."

Hurrah! She had found it: a situation, strength or skill she can call upon and use whenever her power or internal security is challenged. Find your own statement and keep it handy. You'll be surprised how powerful it can be.

Control with Others

Will Schutz, a behavioral scientist who has long studied group behavior, refers to control as "the ability to influence people."

This kind of control can be either positive or negative. When it grows from a persuasive projection of your personal energy it can be motivating and stimulating to the people around you. On the other hand, control that develops from coercive, manipulative and domineering behavior invites passivity, rebellion and malicious compliance.

A negative control style is illustrated by the experience of Ms. James, the president of a retail clothing store. Powerful and aggressive, she runs a tight ship. Recently, she sent four of her department managers to one of our workshops on assertive management because she considered them too weak in dealing with suppliers and salespeople. Ms. James may have had a sound idea, but the way she acted on it had a negative effect on the department managers. The four were "volunteered" by Ms. James, not asked if they wanted to attend the workshop. That soured them on the idea from the beginning. Also, because the workshop was in a nearby city, they were given the afternoon off before the workshop for driving time. Again, a nice idea; but in their mailbox the day before leaving they found a memo from Ms. James saying she hoped they would handle themselves professionally and not stay out late the night before the workshop, because then they wouldn't learn as much and would be wasting the company's money. The managers were insulted, and by now committed to not learning anything — much less the assertive management skills they were sent for.

Such an approach was not unusual for Ms. James; her employees described her as someone who never delegated responsibility to them. She built checkpoints for herself into every task so that she could take the credit when things went well. The employees felt this was a never-ending cycle, and that if she wouldn't let them take some risks and make decisions on their own they would remain dependent and powerless in her eyes, and ultimately in their own.

They also described Ms. James' habit of making changes in policy, prices and products without consulting or informing her department managers. They constantly faced the frustration of wasting time by rechecking every detail and feeling ignorant and out of control.

Throughout the course of the two-day workshop, we analyzed some of the costs of Ms. James' actions. The conclusions: In her attempts to control, she coerced; in her attempts to motivate, she manipulated; and in her attempts to persuade, she alienated. The results were resentment, frustration and anger. If this situation continued, further costs might be lack of motivation, increased insecurity and possibly passive sabotage from the employees.

The four managers were told to ask themselves, "Do I want to continue working under the leadership of Ms. James?" Each did a cost-benefit analysis of her job and came up with many reasons to stay, at least long enough to try to turn around her work relationship with Ms. James.

After this important choice was made we spent considerable time developing an action plan to reeducate Ms. James. The plan included feedback, conflict management, dealing effectively with criticism (they anticipated a bumpy road for a while), setting limits and, of course, positive reinforcement for those things Ms. James was doing right!

Ms. James' management style is not uncommon. Used in the office with workers or in the home with spouse and children, this style depowers people, using humiliation to gain control. People who use this style generally believe that people are idiots and will misbehave if left on their own. They motivate people with fear, criticism and intimidation. If you ever identify this style in people you deal with, you should begin an action reeducation plan immediately — or run as fast as you can! It is impossible to feel personally powerful when a significant person in your life is playing by this depowering set of rules.

Ms. Burgess, head of social science research at a Midwestern university, gets good results using a positive control style. The researchers and research assistants in her department are generally confident, competent and enthusiastic about their work. Ms. Burgess was therefore surprised when Rachel, one of her best research assistants, turned in an assignment on the "underground economy." Not only was the work brought in late, it was incomplete and badly organized.

Ms. Burgess did not react by blaming Rachel; she recognized her poor performance as a signal that something was wrong. But what? Rachel had handled dozens of similar assignments in the past. She should be able to turn out work like this with her eyes closed by now!

Then it hit her: Rachel had done so much of this kind of work, it had ceased to be a challenge. She probably *was* doing it with her eyes closed — falling asleep from boredom. She had compiled data and prepared rough drafts on many topics,always handing her work over to someone else to be written up and published. She might well be bored, and was certainly due for some recognition. Ms. Burgess scheduled a private meeting with Rachel so the two of them could talk it over.

When she brought up the subject of the assignment, Ms. Burgess did not emphasize Rachel's failure, but stressed instead the excellence of her work in general.

"This is not up to your standards, Rachel," she said. "Is there a problem?"

Ms. Burgess' guess proved correct. Rachel was suffering from a lack of motivation, and had been having trouble keeping her mind on her work. When Ms. Burgess suggested that she complete her research on the underground economy and then write the paper by herself, Rachel was excited.

"Will my name be on the article? I'll get full credit?" she asked.

Yes, Ms. Burgess assured her, she would receive full credit for the article when it was published by the university press. If Rachel had any questions about the project, she would be glad to help.

The plan worked; Ms. Burgess was glad to see Rachel motivated and enthusiastic again. The article on the underground economy was well-researched and well-written, and earned Rachel a promotion to researcher. Rachel, Ms. Burgess and the department all benefited. Ms. Burgess' only regret was that, because of her own involvement in other work, she hadn't made better use of Rachel's abilities earlier.

Ms. Burgess is an effective manager because she is able to motivate people by bringing out their best qualities. She empowers the people in her department to stretch their limits, and rewards them for work well done.

As Rachel put it: "Before I worked for Ms. Burgess I was timid about my ability. I might have refused to take on all the responsibility for the article and just kept doing the same job, compiling research for other people, even though I was bored. And another boss might have demoted me when my work began to slide, instead of trusting me to try something more difficult. But Ms. Burgess makes me feel just like the Little Engine who pulls the train up the mountain in the children's story. I don't say "I'm tired," or "It's too hard" anymore; I hear myself saying "I think I can, I think I can," all the way through a project. I end up succeeding — and it's great!"

Control Style A (Depowering)

An individual who uses Control Style A manages people by:
- Overinstructing or underinstructing for tasks
- Refusing to delegate authority with responsibility
- Insisting on being included in all decisions
- **Denying staff** participation in decision-making; changing **mind** without consulting employees

And motivates people with:
- Fear
- Criticism
- Intimidation
- Menial tasks
- Constant checks on work

Underlying Message: "If you don't do things my way, your replacement will!"

Control Style B (Empowering)

An individual who uses Control Style B manages people by:
- Instructing and monitoring according to the skill level of the employee
- Delegating authority with responsibility

- Including staff participation in decision-making, consulting others before making changes
- Giving access to resources and facilitating information

And motivates people with:
- Praise
- Challenging tasks
- Visibility
- Recognition
- Trust in their ability

Underlying message: "You are a valuable resource and I respect, encourage and promote your growth."

Skills

Skills are next on the personal power star. Mastery of people skills and technical skills is essential to personal power. On several occasions people have been sent to us with an introduction like: "she is a great engineer but she sure needs to learn how to handle her subordinates better."

For newly appointed managers or those interested in pursuing the management track, learning how to get things done through other people is a must; that's what the word *management* means. There are five major management functions: planning, organizing, directing, controlling and evaluating. The aspiring manager should be committed to enhancing her performance in each of these areas.

Through each of these functions is woven the thread of effective communication, or people, skills. Rosabeth Moss Kanter, professor in organization sociology and management at Yale University, states that position, not leadership style, is the key variable to accessing power inside organization structures. She describes the ability to get cooperation from other people as the second skill necessary for achieving and maintaining power. Personal power as we've described it, therefore, brings us to position power. Once we have attained position power, we use personal power, through people skills, to get things done.

We, the authors, consider the following to be the primary communication skills for increasing personal power:

1. Listening — the ability to listen to the words and hear the message behind the words. The ability to deepen a conversation to prompt more information and to truly understand all of what is being said. "I hear you saying you are not pleased with your assignment. Could you please tell me specifically what parts of the assignment bother you?"
2. Speaking clearly and directly — the ability to deliver a clear statement with no hidden messages. We must understand our own feelings and motivations in order to clarify and send direct messages. "I want the annual report completed by noon Friday with additional copies for the members of the board."
3. Verbal and nonverbal congruence — the ability to support verbal statements with nonverbal behaviors that deliver the same message. "I feel frustrated that the budget variation was due this morning and it has still not arrived." (Said with look of frustration, knitted brow, stern mouth, straight face.)
4. Setting limits — the ability to set priorities and refuse to spend time on things and people that interfere with those priorities. "I won't be able to chair the Red Cross meeting this year. With my new job responsibilities and the children I don't have the time I used to for volunteer activity."
5. Making requests — the ability to ask clearly, persistently and persuasively for the things we want. "I want to receive a 10 percent increase above this year's wage increase. My duties and responsibilities have far exceeded my job description in the following ways, and I feel my work contribution justifies a salary increase."
6. Managing conflict — the ability to sort through the facts, behaviors and feelings of a difficult situation. In managing conflict it is especially important to separate facts from assumptions and present feelings from prior history. "I am

aware that you arrived thirty-five minutes late for the staff meeting this morning. I felt frustrated not having your input on the Anderson project that was discussed in the first half hour."

Managing conflict is a two-way communication process, and the sender of the message should always wait to hear the perceptions and feelings of the recipient. The next step is to move on to what we want the other person to do. "I would appreciate your filling me in now on your opinion of the Anderson project, and I want you to be on time for Monday's meeting."

7. Negotiating — the ability to give and take. Negotiating requires entering situations with a clear idea of what you want and what you don't want, as well as paying attention to the needs, concerns and interests of the other party.

8. Motivating — the ability to assess what is important to the people around you. Praise, reward, compliments, money, recognition, visibility and feedback are all excellent motivators. It takes observation and assessment to choose the one that best meets the needs of each of your employees. Ken Blanchard, a management consultant and author of the best selling *The One Minute Manager,* says the best motivator is "catching people doing things right. We so often give people attention when they do things wrong that the process of catching people doing things right will actually stimulate them to behave in that positive direction again and again."

People skills can be identified, analyzed, taught, learned and mastered. Practice and experience with these skills can increase your position of power, and in using them you will also empower others.

Technical Expertise

Betty Harragan states in *Games Mother Never Taught You* that skills are the bottom line for women in business. We agree — without skills you're not even on the power chart. Technical skills, by the same token, can be looked at as the access point to the power star. If one has nothing else, no confidence, decisiveness, control or awareness, skills can be the starting point.

Make sure you are fully aware of at least the minimum requirements in your given field to obtain the job, pay and recognition you want. There are enough ways that women get discriminated against in organizational structures — don't let the basic skill requirements be one of them for you. While working with a large government agency, we dealt with a group of women who complained that they were not given the same opportunities as the men because the information on in-house training courses was passed out on the supervisory level. Therefore, if they didn't have a good working relationship with their supervisor, they received the information too late to apply for the courses necessary for promotion. Many of these practices are changing, but sometimes the changes are slow. Be proactive and initiate conversations with significant people to make sure they know your career goals and will pass relevant information on to you.

Technical expertise can also increase your power with people who carry negative stereotypes of women. Let's say you are a pioneer in a male-dominated field and often feel the scrutiny of your male counterparts. The only way to be accepted into the ranks is through your skill and competence. Many of the men may still treat you like their mother, kid sister or wife, but a few smart ones will soon begin to recognize your knowledge and skills. The trick is to persistently and calmly lead with your technical expertise. After being accepted as a contributing member of the team you will dramatically expand your power base because now you are recognized as having something of value to give — your skills.

Awareness

The major accomplishment of the early Feminist movement was to increase awareness of what it means to be a woman in our society. Once the issues were understood, change could be effected. Paulo Friere, a South American educator who has illuminated the dynamics of oppression, says that powerless people need to develop a critical consciousness that questions, challenges, explores and investigates *what is* in order to bring about *what should be.*

To analyze more effectively, we have separated awareness into two types: personal and political.

Personal Awareness

Our first challenge is to be aware of ourselves physically, emotionally, mentally and spiritually. To maintain an empowering level of personal awareness we need time each day for introspection and reflection. We need uninterrupted time (even if it's just fifteen minutes each morning and evening) to ask ourselves such questions as:

- How am I doing?
- How do I feel?
- Am I holding any tensions? If so, what are they from?
- What do I want to do today?
- What have I done today to achieve my goals?
- Do I need to clear up any problems in any of my personal or professional relationships?
- Do I feel nurtured, cared for, appreciated? If not, what can I do to get these for myself?

Once you've gained awareness of yourself in this manner, try some systematic relaxation exercises to calm and clear your mind. Regularly followed, these exercises can provide welcome relief in a busy, overcommitted lifestyle.

The only person who can effectively direct and channel your resources is you. And your resources — your time, your skills and your energy — are the roots of your personal power. It is absolutely necessary for you to be aware of the way in which you allocate your resources to those around you. A structured awareness process also helps you to deal with your problems as they arise. When we try to ignore them — or are unaware — they surface months later in disease and burnout. We've done a great deal of work with women who experience burnout. When asked when the first symptoms of anxiety, depression, loss of interest and conflicts appeared they replied it had been several months before. When asked how they reacted to this early awareness, they invariably admit that they ignored the symptoms and pushed themselves even harder in order to cope. This process ultimately cost them much more in time and energy than if they had acted on their real feelings in the first place.

Political Awareness

Our second challenge is to be aware of the culture and politics of the systems in which we live and work.

In a group of two or a group of two thousand, certain dynamics develop around norms, boundaries, leaders, history, ethics, physical environment, process, function and goals. The primary responsibility of today's professional woman is to be aware of how these dynamics affect her life. Skills that create success in one milieu bring failure in another. The identity of a firm can range from supercharged overdrive to bureaucratic caution. Only through a conscious understanding of your organizational culture can you be assured that you are not a victim of hidden actions and influences or a cultural misfit. It can be a painful experience to be a highly energized producer stuck in the middle of a bureaucratic system being told repeatedly to be patient and slow down! Think about it. There just might be another cultural environment that is starving for your high energy and willingness to take risks.

Sophisticated systems of racism, sexism, ageism and culturism are all inherent in American institutions and corporations. The aware woman knows where, when and how these get played out in her organization. Affirmative action has altered the American work place, but it is your task to alter the spirit. Here is a list of some questions that will help you develop an effective awareness of your work environment.

The Culture of Your Organization

- Who are the leaders in your organization?
- Are men and women treated alike or differently?
- Do they have similar or different opportunities?
- What is the highest position held by a woman?
- What is the ratio of men to women in positions of leadership and power?
- What is the language used to describe work roles? (Example: policeman/police officer)
- What is the dress code of those in positions of leadership and power?
- Are men/women called by first or last names?
- Where do individuals eat? Congregate?
- With whom?
- What are the ages, race, gender of those individuals in upper management?
- Middle management?
- Lower management?
- What are the styles and ages of female support staff? (Are only young, cheerleader types hired? Or matronly, experienced, mother types?)
- How are emotions expressed? (Affection, anger, approval, disapproval)
- What are the rules of your organization regarding promotion, leaves, hiring, firing?
- How do men and women behave toward each other?

The Politics of Your Organization

- Who has the legitimate power? (Title and role)
- Who has the real power?
- Who do you go to when you want a decision made?
- A decision implemented?
- Who talks to whom?
- Who is campaigning for what position?

- How does your organization determine promotions? (By majority, by appointment, by default, by assignment)
- What criteria do they use? (Skills, looks, a preferred race, age, culture, sex; track record, competence)
- Who are the conservatives, liberals, independents?
- Who supports you?
- What are their positions?
- Whom do you support?
- What are their positions?
- Are members of the Black, Asian, native American and white races represented in your organization?
- What roles and positions do they hold?
- Are members of different ethnic groups represented in your organization?
- What roles and positions do they hold?

The above questions are designed to increase your awareness of elements that are influencing your status at work. To the degree that you are aware of these influences, you will successfully avoid being victimized by them. You will also be able to strategically combat any sexist, racist, and ageist practices while developing yourself as a powerful, empowering woman.

2. Sex-Role Stereotypes

Years of striving for professional success have supplied me with an abundance of feedback on my behavior, both solicited and unsolicited. I have surely received my share of criticism for not complying with the stereotyped expectations for women's behavior. Now, when I look back on it, it is clear to me that my behavior wasn't necessarily wrong; it just didn't go along with who I was expected to be. But at the time, those criticisms were as confusing to me as they seemed clarifying to the people who made them.

I was labeled too competitive *when I volunteered to take charge of a certain project. The woman who made the remark told me I should have waited until someone nominated me. (I might still be waiting there if I'd taken her advice.)*

I was labeled hostile *by two men in a newly formed work group when I expressed my displeasure with their raised voices, shaking fists and threatening remarks. One of them told me later that he had been planning to ask me out, but changed his mind because of my comments. (Apparently that was supposed to send me home regretting my behavior.)*

Another time, when I suggested a change in procedure to accommodate expressed employee needs, the reply I received was "Arleen, we have a job to do here." My concerns, dismissed as "too sensitive and too soft," were seen as interfering with the task at hand rather than addressing issues relevant to how the task should be done.

I am still hearing the comment that disturbs me most of all. When my performance has pleased and surprised someone, I will often be told that I am different; a unique kind of woman. I insist on refuting that statement — it's not a compliment to me, but a reassurance to the speaker that he/or she need not abandon stereotyped views of women in general.

— AL

Several years ago, when I began training groups of managers, and 75 to 80 percent of the trainees were men, I experienced much greater anxiety and self-doubt than when training women. Realizing I had a problem, I consulted with a friend, Pat. Our conversation went like this:

Pat: What do you think these men are thinking when you're teaching?

Me: They're wondering what a woman is doing telling them about managing people. They don't think I have the expertise to be teaching them and they ignore what I have to say because I'm a woman and not a man.

Pat: Do you know any men that feel you're competent, bright and capable?

Me: Yes, two that come to mind immediately are my husband, Rich Goodstein and my boss, Rob Rutherford. And then there are several friends I've known for years.

Pat: Do you respect and accept their opinion?

Me: Of course I do.

Pat: Then, for a while, I want you to mentally change the faces of the men in your workshops to those of Rich and Rob and your men friends.

Initially, it sounded gimmicky to me, but I thought I'd give it a try. During visualization and practice for my programs, I started to imagine a room full of men that I knew were respectful of my abilities and skills. Eventually I felt my attitude toward

*my work changing. I started to feel more positive and more con-
fident before my presentations. The workshops became more
effective, and the managers began asking questions more frequently (a sign to me they accepted and wanted my opinions).*

*After about six months, I was cured. I had successfully
changed the negative stereotype I had formerly carried of the
men in my groups to a positive one. I was more relaxed, less
defensive and much more open to the men in my groups as individuals, treating them the way I wanted them to treat me.*

— DAL

Sally

Once upon a time a little girl was born. Her parents named
her Sally. She was laid to sleep in a crib painted with a pink
bunny, tucked in with a pretty pink blanket. Sally was cuddled,
handled gingerly and told she was ever so cute. She was given
pretty dresses, fine tea sets, plenty of dolls and a carriage to push
them in. She was taught to be polite, coy, deferent and seen but
not heard. She was encouraged to play with her dollhouse, stay
close to home and bake with her toy oven. Later on she helped
mommy with the housework on Saturdays and accompanied her
as she cooked the family meal each evening. Sally was a very
cooperative little girl, who received much praise for her role as
"mommy's little helper."

Some of Sally's favorite childhood activities were cut-outs,
sewing, needlework and taking care of the needs of her many,
many dolls. She had a great deal of responsibility keeping them
all clothed and groomed. Sally's parents knew the benefits of
physical education, so they sent her to dancing school, where she
got plenty of exercise while successfully avoiding the perils of

tomboyhood. Sally wore her tutu and ballet slippers with pride, and was careful to keep them clean.

As Sally grew older she became an avid reader, seeking out adventure and fun through the exploits of Nancy Drew, Cherry Ames and the Bobsey twins. She couldn't wait until high school, when she could become a cheerleader. She fantasized about cheering the team on to victory from the sidelines, and thought if she were very lucky, she, like the girl who lived across the street, would someday date a football player. By the time she actually entered high school she had plans to have at least four children — she already had their names picked out.

High school offered all kinds of excitement: cheerleading, school dances, service clubs, hours spent in front of the mirror and boys, boys, boys! In between there were studies and talk of future plans. Sally's guidance counselor advised her not to take chemistry; since it was a difficult subject it might jeopardize her honor roll status. She complied and soon went off to college with honor grades to pursue a degree in social work — a choice her peers and teachers found admirable.

John

Once upon a time a little boy was born. His parents named him John. He was laid to sleep in a crib painted with a blue teddy bear, snugly tucked in with a little blue blanket. Johnny was jostled and hugged and bounced about. He giggled and yelped with glee when his father threw him high into the air. He received footballs before he could hold them, as well as baseballs, bats, soldiers, tanks, trucks, cowboys, erector sets, Lincoln Logs and dungarees. Sometimes Johnny got into trouble, made too much noise and got into fights, but as his father often said while shaking his head, "boys will be boys."

As Johnny grew older much of his time was spent playing Little League baseball and Pee Wee football. He learned very early the rules of good sportsmanship and received much recognition, praise and attention from peers and parents for his accomplishments. The family often gathered to watch and cheer Johnny and his team on to victory. As a result, Johnny became an avid competitor and learned early the rewards of winning.

In high school, sports brought an added benefit — the admiration of girls. Being in the limelight sure could be fun! John (as he now preferred to be called) soon learned to accept, even expect, attention and devotion.

For his academic courses, John took chemistry, physics, mechanical drawing and all the math his schedule could hold. After all, his guidance counselor said, he had to prepare for a career.

Social Programming

Are these scenes familiar to you? The tragedy of conventional child rearing practices is that the beliefs about who we are and who we can grow to be are programmed from birth — long before there is a possibility of conscious choice.

For example, if parents, teachers and society all say little girls become nurses while little boys become doctors, what child would argue? A child hears the statements as truth and patterns his or her life to fit the expectations. Of course there are exceptions, but ask anyone who has successfully bucked social expectations and you will hear a story of struggle, determination and overcompensation that would challenge the strongest of wills.

The social programming that sends girls in one direction and boys in another is called sex-role conditioning. Sex-role conditioning leads to another phenomenon that further directs our choices in life: *sex-role stereotyping.*

Bailey Jackson III, and Rita Hardiman, of New Perspectives, a New England-based consulting firm on racism and sexism, outline the characteristics of stereotyping in the following way:

• Someone outside of the group does the labeling of the stereotype. For example, those people dedicated to dealing with women's issues call themselves feminists. Others call them women's libbers, as in "Oh, no, you're not one of those women's libbers, are you?"

- Usually negative qualities are noticed and are used to confine or limit. "She is so emotional I'm sure she won't be able to handle the pressure of a management position."
- A stereotype usually contains an element of truth, small or large; however the element is exaggerated, generalized to other members of the group, and often taken out of context. "Frankly I'm against hiring another woman engineer for the research department. The last one stayed only two years before she got pregnant and took time off. We can't afford that kind of work record around here."

Some adjectives commonly used to stereotype women are: sweet, loving, kind, passive, helpful, short-sighted, nurturing and emotional. Typical stereotypes for men are: strong, decisive, assertive, independent, result-oriented, critical and rational. Of course, not all women fall into the first category or all men into the second; but most of the time these labels are thought to be representative of some part of reality. This is precisely where a stereotype gets its power — because some of the time it does fit. However, problems arise when it's looked at as the whole truth rather than a partial truth at best. There are many independent, assertive women and there are many caring, nurturing men. And many people of both sexes are independent, nurturing, assertive *and* caring. Few of us actually have such lopsided personalities that we follow either stereotype exclusively. But then why do we feel, deep inside, that we *should* resemble the stereotype of our sex? If the stereotypes are damaging and demonstrably unrealistic, then why are they so pervasive in our culture?

To begin with, socialization is a lot stronger in the early years than many of us think. Current research shows that after the age of six months boys are picked up and hugged less than girls. Marc Feigen Fasteau, in his book *The Male Machine*, states that the gap widens as children grow older, with boys being discouraged from asking for attention and pressured toward autonomy. How many times have you observed a parent telling a little boy to be brave when he hurt himself? "Only little girls and sissies cry," is the common saying. Girls, however, learn the exact opposite. In studies of kindergarden children, girls are talked to more than boys and are encouraged to stay closer to the teacher.

Selma Greenberg, author of *Right From the Start: A Nonsexist Approach To Child Rearing*, states that by age three children often wish to play with and be with only those people and things that they have been taught are appropriate to their sex. She relates a study done by Lisa Serbin and Jane Connor, research psychologists on sex-role issues. Serbin and Connor placed toys, each typically associated with either boys or girls, in a room. When a single child entered and remained alone, he or she chose toys linked with both sexes. When another child entered, the child being observed chose "sex-appropriate" toys. Just being in the presence of the second child inhibited the curiosity and exploration of the first. Peer pressure subtly applied served to remind the child of what was off-limits play! This study is illustrated by the story of a woman who dared to challenge the implicit rules of sex-role play as a child. In her kindergarden class there was a great collection of building blocks, much better than those she had at home, which she coveted. They were, however, considered to be the boys' territory. When she finally got up the courage to sit down and build a castle with them, she was forcibly removed by the teacher — a woman! — who directed her to the doll corner with the warning, "blocks are not for girls."

The media is a major influence on young minds. Think back to the television of the late fifties and sixties; there were very clear roles for men and women to follow. *Ozzie and Harriet, Father Knows Best* (just the title says enough), *Lassie, My Three Sons,* and *Leave it to Beaver* all portrayed situations where the men went to work and the women stayed home as mothers and caretakers. Very few career options were depicted for young women. Those that *were* shown — in *Hazel, Our Miss Brooks* and *The Ann Sothern Show* — portrayed women in traditional jobs of housekeeper, teacher and secretary. Young men, on the other hand, could choose from a wide range of occupations: doctor (*Ben Casey* and *Dr. Kildare*), lawyer (*Perry Mason*), policeman (*Dragnet*), factory worker (*The Life of Riley*), bus driver (Jackie Gleason), band leader (Desi Arnaz), private eye (*77 Sunset Strip*), adventurer (*Route 66*), cowboy (*Gunsmoke*). The options were endless.

As if this weren't enough, Saturday morning cartoonland offered more of the same. We saw Popeye saving Olive Oyl, Fred Flintstone being fed by Wilma and Mrs. Jetson spending George's money after cracking up the family car (oh, those women drivers!). Even though *Wonder Woman* and *Sesame Street* have finally arrived on the American TV scene, the men running corporate America were raised on the earlier, sexist shows — and so were their sisters.

Anyway, the eighties aren't free from sex stereotyping either. Even in *E. T., the Extraterrestrial,* Hollywood's success of the century, Eliot, his brother, and their schoolboy friends rode bicycles into the wild blue yonder as Gertie stood watching at her mother's side.

Literature for children typically presents the same dynamics between men and women. Picture the fairytale princess waiting patiently and passively for the prince to come. And remember good, beautiful Cinderella working her fingers to the bone while her stepmother and lazy sisters watched? Thank heavens she was finally rescued by the handsome prince and saved from further drudgery! And how about Goldilocks, a curious, independent little girl who dares to venture out to explore and expand her horizons? She would have been eaten by a bear if she hadn't escaped just in time and run home to her mother —it's not hard to find the moral of that story! Think back to fairy tales and stories of your childhood. Can you identify a strong, assertive, creative or resourceful female role model? Aside from the wonderful Pipi Longstocking, none comes to mind (except of course the mean, ugly witches and stepmothers, who further reinforce the message that "good girls know their place.") Both sexes have been hurt by these stereotypes, because the formula is so rigid.

For women: be passive, sweet and hard working. Don't be pushy, and someone will come along to rescue and reward you. For men: be strong, silent, wealthy (if you don't own a kingdom, forget it) and independent. Go after what you want, and you will be rewarded with a passive, devoted, loving woman. It's no wonder we're experiencing a time of role conflict and transition, with both sexes feeling betrayed and confused.

The crux of the sex-role problem arises when the descriptive statement becomes a prescriptive statement: doctors are male, nurses are female. The illogical conclusion is: therefore, doctors should be male, nurses should be female. Society believes this, parents believe this, teachers believe this and so do little girls and little boys! In the USSR, sex-role conditioning, at least in the medical professions, is very different. 75 percent of Russian doctors are women. The tenacious roots of sex-role conditioning are culture-bound and depend on child rearing, educational, social, religious and ethnic practices and beliefs.

The underlying critical issue that surfaces when discussing sex-role differences is that of power. As a point of illustration, let's look at the doctor-nurse dynamic. For anyone who has spent time in a hospital it is quite clear who is in the position of greater power. Staff nurses earn an average income of $17,000; physicians earn an average income of $74,500. These figures represent quite a differential in earning potential, and are indicative of nurses' and doctors' respective access to other sources of power.

As an example, corporate suites are filled with white men, groomed since birth for exactly these positions. It is this youthful conditioning that sets the stage for the continuing power differential. We are used to seeing the pretty cheerleader urging her boyfriend on to victory from the sidelines, so it seems to us harmless enough — until we look at the implications for her life. As an adult, *she* is the corporate wife or secretary, and *he* is the chief executive officer. Not a far cry from the playing field — she's cheering and he's winning.

Feminists tell us that when we are exposed to situations where the balance of power is distorted along sex lines we should ask the question, "who benefits?"

Ask yourself that question about this example: Joanne, a geophysicist with a large gas and oil exploration firm in the Midwest, was sent to attend a professional development course we were conducting. She was pleased with her job, earned a good wage and felt powerful because she had successfully entered a male-dominated field. During the course of the workshop she described a company policy that upset her somewhat: Women could not go into the field unattended. She considered this a silly rule, but she had been told by her superiors that it was for her own benefit. There could be an accident, they explained, or some unfortunate, embarrassing incident might occur with the men in the field, who were not used to women geophysicists. As we explored the situation, the question arose: Who *really* benefits from such a policy? Not Joanne. Who could respect her as a powerful individual when she couldn't even go on field trips alone? Who would ever consider promoting such a professional? No one! That one "silly" rule effectively shut Joanne out of the running. As in many other cases, the ostensible gallantry of "protecting" a member of the so-called weaker sex resulted in keeping women in their place — a place of lesser importance. This single factor was ultimately much more damaging to Joanne's career than she had originally thought.

Rosabeth Moss Kanter, in *Men and Women of the Corporation*, talks about two stereotypes that block women's access to power in organizational settings. The first is "no one wants to work for a woman;" the second, "women are too bossy and controlling to make good leaders anyway."

In reference to the "no one wants to work for a woman" syndrome, Kanter explains that subordinates want to work for people who have power already; managers who are winners can take subordinates along on their way to the top. At present most people with these characteristics are men. A recent article from *Ms* magazine discusses this issue, offering the example of a woman news manager from a local TV station. After attaining the position she found herself isolated. "There have been very few upper-level jobs open to women," she states, "so there was a lot of jealousy. The hostility was collective. Part of the reason was that women were used to getting what they wanted out of a male boss — I think they felt they couldn't get anything out of me because I'm a young woman. But I began to work for them; I got them good assignments. That helped change their attitude."

The second stereotype, "women are too bossy and controlling to make good leaders," is often reflected to us by women in our workshops. One woman's statement is similar to Kanter's description. She says, "Woman bosses are too particular, too controlling. They want to watch over everything you're doing and can get downright bitchy about details. I'd work for a man any day — he gives the orders and lets me do things my way."

One way to look at this stereotype is that women aren't used to having people work for us. Therefore, we need to master the art of delegating, encouraging people to function on their own. Another way to look at this is that women aren't used to female bosses and therefore have difficulty dealing with them. An executive secretary described the following incident to us. Her female boss rushed in from a meeting, handed her a handwritten report and told her she needed it typed immediately and copied for the board meeting that evening. The secretary was very disgruntled that she hadn't even been asked if she had time to do the report, or at least talked to in a less aggressive manner. I asked her to imagine a male boss behaving in exactly the same way; would she still feel so offended and put off? She thought for a minute and said no — it was OK for a male boss to be aggressive, but she somehow expected more politeness and sensitivity from a female boss. What we have here is a double stereotype — "women are too bossy to be bosses," coupled with "women should be more sensitive and polite." Possibly women are looked at as being too bossy because people *expect* them to be sensitive and nurturing. When a woman departs from her stereotype everyone has difficulty relating to her! If women are to survive in the corporate world, we must be granted the opportunity to be bosses; and we must be able to act like bosses, and be granted our managerial behavior.

The following sex-role stereotypes are used with the permission of Rosabeth Moss Kanter, based on material from *Men and Women of the Corporation* (New York, Basic Books, 1977), and *A Tale of "O"; On Being Different* (New York, Harper & Row, 1980, and videotape from Goodmeasure, Inc., P.O. Box 3004, Cambridge, Mass. 02139). We have added to Kanter's role descriptions a list of the skills women can use to break out of these stereotypes. We are grateful to the women who have participated in our workshops for sharing their ideas and giving us insight into the workings of the following roles.

Mother

Stereotype	*Personally Powerful Woman*
1. Puts others first, doesn't promote self enough	Owns and promotes competence, skills and accomplishments
2. Waits to be noticed	Asks for what she wants — doesn't wait until it's offered
3. Resists setting limits	Says no and sets limits
4. Listens indiscriminately	Sets limits on listening time
5. Interferes in others' conflicts; plays the peace maker	Sets emotional boundaries with other employees, manages conflicts effectively
6. Overinstructs if she is a domineering mother, underinstructs if she is a permissive one. Others are her priority	Teaches coworkers to question and explore alternatives themselves; delegates
7. Gives advice (even when not asked)	Gives feedback
8. Fosters dependence	Fosters independence

The office mother gives recognition, but doesn't seek it for herself. She works behind the scenes to promote others' success. You can spot her quite easily — she's the one that makes coffee for everyone else, and cleans up after them.

Seductress

Stereotype	*Personally Powerful Woman*
1. Uses sexuality to get what she wants with provocative body language (gesture, postures, walk)	Uses brains, competence and communication skills to get what she wants
2. Dresses in tight or revealing clothes accentuating the figure	Chooses appropriate professional dress
3. Flirts to be included with men	Finds common ground for conversation with men
4. Uses men for primary support system	Includes women in support system
5. Manipulates and vies for male attention	Performs tasks and responsibilities effectively for recognition

There are times when the seductress is ostracized by the women in her organization. A woman can be labeled a seductress by men who are attracted to her. This is their way of not taking responsibility for their attraction to her. Kanter says this is the one role in which a woman can be labeled, yet not be manifesting any of the behaviors of the label.

Pet, Cheerleader, Office Mascot

Stereotype	*Skills to remove Stereotype*
1. Acts cute and cheerful, no matter how she feels	Is congruent emotionally (can be playful, angry or creative, depending on the situation)
2. Disowns power, skills and strengths; usually promotes men	States strengths assertively Promotes self and others of both sexes
3. Dresses in ruffles, bows, and fluff	Assesses professional look in the organization and dresses accordingly
4. Social director: organizes office parties (Christmas, birthdays, retirement, etc.)	Cooperates as a team member in social functions
5. Compliments too often for too little reason	Compliments only for a job well done, is specific and genuine in her compliments; promotes self
6. Compliant, overly agreeable and cheerful; Pollyanna attitude — everything is always "wonderful"	Disagrees when necessary Competes when necessary
7. Can be just like one of the guys	Sets own priorities; recognizes the uniqueness of who she is
8. People are surprised when she says something bright	Knows her strengths and uses them; doesn't hide them in order to be included

Iron Maiden, Queen Bee

Stereotype	*Personally Powerful Woman*
1. Rigid in her boundaries with others; no talk of personal life	Willing to confide safe personal things
2. Dresses like an army colonel	Comfortable with her femininity
3. Sets serious "business only" tone at all times	Uses humor and some small talk to enrich conversation while maintaining professionalism
4. Is often more critical than complimentary	Gives specific compliments for job well done
5. Thinks people should pull themselves up by bootstraps, as she did	Empowers others with mentor/sponsor roles
6. Often aggressive, cold and unapproachable	Assesses relationships on individual basis
7. Would rather compete than collaborate with own team members	Knows her friends and enemies, and responds accordingly

In addition to these stereotypes, we add the Superwoman. She often appears in our workshops seeking some semblance of personal professional balance to an overcommitted, busy life. (For an in-depth discussion of this stereotype, see Chapter 9.)

Superwoman

Stereotype	*Skills to Remove Stereotype*
1. Must do everything herself if it's to be done correctly	Delegates responsibilities to others, trusting that they will handle them
2. Demands perfection	Values others' standards as much as own
3. Overcommits her time, doesn't set limits, thus has little or no personal time	Manages resources effectively (time, skills, energy)
4. Takes on multiple commitments and roles; feels torn and guilty about tradeoffs to balance roles	Makes time to evaluate priorities and goals; chooses roles based on clear values and priorities; reasonably lowers standards for each role when there are many (As Natasha Josefowitz says in her book of poetry *Is this where I was going?* "Everything worth doing is not worth doing well")
5. Often feels isolated; doesn't ask for support from others; resents when no one offers	Requests what she wants; asks for support in proactive manner; doesn't wait for someone to notice she needs it

These roles pose difficulties for the woman when they block her from achieving the full use of her power and potential. They can often appear unconsciously, from years of social conditioning; self-awareness can keep you from falling prey to their pitfalls.

The ultimate goal is to have a balance between traditional male and female behaviors packaged in the same person — in other words, the best of both worlds.

The Best of Both Worlds

The ideal state, in the professional world particularly, is androgyny. Androgyny (from *andro*, male and *gyne*, female) is an archetype that represents the coming together of male and female qualities. In an androgynous situation, men and women could pick and choose those behaviors that best represent their individual personality. The range of human response would be far more creative and flexible, imaginative and spontaneous. An androgynous world would also assure equal opportunities to promote the most basic of human rights — the right for people to choose who they will be.

Sandra Bem, a social psychologist from Stanford University who has done a great deal of sex-role research, sums up the ideal.

> Androgyny allows an individual to be both independent and tender, supportive, yielding, masculine and feminine. Thus, androgyny greatly expands the range of behaviors open to everyone, permitting people to cope more effectively with diverse situations. As such, I hope that androgyny will some day come to define a new and more human standard of psychological health.

Personal Self-Assessment

The purpose of the last part of this chapter is to help you explore and identify your own stereotypes that limit and inhibit who you are. Muriel Goldfarb and Mara Gleckel, psychotherapists who specialize in organizational consulting and affirmative action, believe that before you change anything about yourself you should first consider your past — particularly, what happened to you in your family. The original stereotype of who you are comes from your parents and siblings, through the names, labels and self-images they gave you. An enlightening exercise is to identify those names, labels and self-images from childhood and remember who contributed to their development. Consider the following:

Lillian, a participant in our workshop who is now an executive secretary, remembered being called *tomboy, pushy, aggressive* and *loud* by her parents. Early in life, she got the distinct message that she would not succeed in this world until she curbed these "negative" behaviors. She also remembers her older brother telling her that no boy would go out with her because she was more of a "jock" than the boys were. She spent most of her adolescence trying to be something she didn't feel —pretty, ladylike and appealing to boys — just to gain the approval of family members and peers.

Ruth, a middle-aged black woman who is a manager at a larger computer firm, recalled the split she felt because of the role she carried from her early conditioning. She was raised in a very strict Baptist family, where she was given a great deal of support for church involvement. She was known as *the good girl, the dependable one, the responsible daughter.* Her family believed she would always be the church organist in their hometown. She spoke to our group of the difficulty she felt in convincing her parents she wanted to go away to school. Still, years later, when she returns home to visit she has to ward off questions about when she will return to resume her work with the church.

Marion, an orthopedic surgeon, proves that early labels can be supportive and directive in goal achievement. Her labels were *determined, bossy, helpful, competitive, bright and real smart.* She found these labels to be very useful in managing the pressures and difficulties of medical school.

Now you take time to make a list and answer the following questions:

- What were your names, labels and images while growing up?
- Who were your image builders?
- What are your names, labels and images now?
- Who contributes to building these for you?
- What would you like your names, labels and images to be?
- Who are your role models for these?
- Which names, labels and images from your childhood have you kept?
- Which have you chosen to give up?

Whenever something is given up there is a potential cost. If you were labeled *good little girl* by your parents and *always cooperative* by your husband and children, you might encounter some disapproval if your present goals are to be more decisive and independent. But perhaps more important than the potential cost is the potential gain, so take time to clarify the benefits you may receive by adding new dimensions to your personality.

3. Risk Taking

When Dolores and I started our own business, I felt I was taking a big risk. The risk wasn't in working with Dolores — we had been close friends and had worked together for years before we decided to become formal partners in the Professional Development Institute. But now it was to be a full-time, all-out effort. It meant I would have to resign my position at the college where I'd worked for seven years, and trust that we would be successful on our own.

For years we had dreamed about having our own business. We had worked toward that goal in many ways: expanding our education and expertise, designing new training programs together, coauthoring materials, promoting ourselves as a team, and including one another in as many training contracts as possible. Now we had been offered a large training contract, and there was no doubt that the time was right. We were finally going to have what we had so long wanted, the joy in working together, autonomy and control over our careers, and a financially successful business.

Soon after my excitement bubbled to the surface, it was followed by a surge of anxiety. What if there were no more contracts after this one? What if we couldn't generate enough work to support ourselves? What would I do then, with no business and no college position to rely on? What would happen to our friendship if we failed?

For a while the risks seemed overwhelming. I thought and talked a lot about them. Gradually I became clearer on a couple of things. One was that my style in preparing myself for risk-taking is to rehearse the worst. When I play out in my head the worst possible outcomes, it helps me let go of the fear. It seems to help me feel that there will be no horrible surprise lurking in unseen corners. By imagining the worst, I feel I can have some control over it, and therefore venture forward more confidently.

I also remembered that I wouldn't be alone in this risk. The major risks in Dolores' and my careers were taken by knowing we had the support of one another. Greater risk would be to deny the strength of our relationship and our ability to succeed.

— AL

Several years ago Rob Rutherford, a well-known seminar leader, contacted me about an assertiveness class I conducted at a local education program. He said he taught assertiveness training on a national level and would like to get together and discuss the material with me. After several meetings, he asked if I wanted to do a section of his program in his New York City seminar. His only concern was that the groups would be considerably larger than I was used to working with (forty-one was my largest count). It was not my style to take risks, and working in New York City with large groups of people felt risky to me. After much consternation, I agreed to do a forty-five-minute section of the workshops. My first group was 175 secretaries in New York City, and the day went well. I was elated: this was easy, I thought. Why had I been so panicked? The following day I spoke with 150 managers. I stood up, saw all those faces, and froze. I couldn't string a sentence together, I fumbled, rambled, got lost, was dry-mouthed and shaky. I finally opened up the presentation to questions, and thank heaven, people were kind enough to ask a couple. I managed to regain a bit of my composure, enough at least to turn the program back over to Rob. One feedback sheet at the end of the day said I was worthless! I was humiliated and mortified — how could I have bungled something I knew so well? I promised myself I would go back home, be satisfied with teaching at the local night school and never venture out again.

When the seminar was over, I met with Rob. He asked if I wanted to join his staff. Although I had a lot to learn, he said, if I was willing, he thought I could do it. I felt if Rob was willing to risk by asking me to work with him, I could at least give it a try. I'm grateful to him to this day for the confidence he placed in me.

As soon as I agreed, an amazing thing happened to me — I had the overwhelming feeling that in order to succeed I would have to make a commitment to myself to go into training. I had images of the Boston marathon and the need for daily concentration and practice to master the skills necessary for entering a new field — one drastically more demanding than the one I would be leaving. It felt like the greatest risk I had ever taken! I knew one thing for sure — I did not know how to do what I agreed to learn to do. My whole life I had gone very cautiously and slowly from one thing to the next, always being sure I could do the next step well before venturing out. I liked being on solid ground. Risk was not a part of my personal or professional life or vocabulary.

Well, it worked — or rather, I worked it. I observed and listened and practiced, and found something very valuable as a result of my training — a new-found confidence in myself and in other people. I finally understood and believed that if I did something long enough and hard enough it would work. I could do it! Previously, I had thought that skills were attributable to inborn talents; people who were good at things were good at them by nature. I had never believed practice and determination could count for so much! Recently, a woman approached me after a workshop and said "You're just a natural at this — I'll never be able to do what you do." Hogwash! I told her she should have been in New York.

— DAL

Picture this: You are attending a department meeting. Your boss has just finished praising your project team for coming up with a new marketing strategy. He announces that the regional meeting, to be held in two weeks, would be an ideal time to outline the strategy for a larger section of the organization. He envisions a formal presentation to about one hundred people, describing the details of the strategy, clarifying its implementation and forecasting the results, with a question-and-answer session to follow. He turns directly to you and your team members and asks "Which of you would like to make the presentation?"

What do you do?

If you're like most of us, you become aware that your heart is beating faster. You feel the tightening sensation in your stomach that means you're excited or anxious. One part of you is challenged, eager to grab hold of this opportunity to be noticed, to represent your team and to be associated with a valuable contribution. Within that part of you, a voice is emerging — a voice on the verge of exclaiming, "I'll do it!" But that voice is quickly hushed by the part of you that is experiencing terror at the thought of standing in front of a crowd. The stress and anxiety would be tremendous. All the time and energy it would take to prepare — overwhelming. The first voice argues back that the visibility would be a great bonus to your career; it would give you credibility and a name in your organization. Should you or shouldn't you? Can you pull it off? You think you could, but what if you couldn't? If only there were a way to be sure.

But there isn't. That's what risking is all about — no guarantees; the possibility exists for either loss or gain. A risk that successfully accomplishes an out-of-the-ordinary task or advances the goals of your organization will gain recognition and power for you. On the other hand, a risk that fails can slow down, and in some cases, altogether destroy your chances for future advancement.

For women in the work place, the dimensions of risk are emphasized. If we don't take any risks, we go unnoticed. Our skills and competencies are often overshadowed by the contrast of our femaleness against a male-dominated environment. If we take a risk and lose, it is seen by some as evidence that we just "haven't got what it takes." Even a small mistake can be perceived as proof that women in general have no business competing with men.

On the other hand, if we take a risk and win, we may reap more benefits than a man who has made a similar accomplishment. Recent research indicates that nothing succeeds like success, especially for women. When a woman becomes established in her field, she may actually be perceived more positively than a man in the same position. Abramson, Goldberg and Abramson call this The Talking Platypus Phenomenon. "When an individual achieves a level of success not anticipated, his/her achievement tends to be magnified rather than diminished. After all, it matters little what the platypus says, the wonder is that it can say anything at all."

Aside from the potential benefits to your career, taking risks can enhance your sense of personal power. Choosing to act despite your fears increases your self-esteem and builds self-confidence. You experience yourself as having courage and independence. Meeting new challenges encourages a feeling of mastery and a greater sense of control over the direction of your life. You find that you can be proactive — someone who initiates and determines the course of events — rather than being reactive to the lead of other people and outside occurrences. At the heart of personal power is the knowledge that you are in charge of your life and have the ultimate responsibility for how you live it. Whether you win or lose at risk-taking, there will always be the knowledge that you decided, you acted, you exercised your power as a human being consciously and actively to influence your environment.

Yet for many women, the reluctance to take a risk persists. When we asked several women to tell us what got in their way of taking risks, we discovered their responses fell into two main categories: fear of failure, and fear of success. It's ironic but true. Let's take a closer look at some typical explanations women make for avoiding risks.

Fear of Failure

Explanation 1: "Just when I get myself psyched up to really go for it, I start to imagine the obstacles and difficulties in my way. Before I know it, those obstacles have gained such power that they dominate my thinking — and all I can see is disaster."

According to Henning and Jardim, in their book *The Managerial Woman*, men understand both sides of risk, the possibility of gain and the possibility of loss, while women are mainly in touch with the negative side — we often see risk as inevitably ending in ruin, injury, hurt and loss. Risk, therefore, is something to avoid. It's not clear why this difference exists, but it seems to arise out of women's sense of powerlessness. Having been for so long denied access to decision-making and policy formulation, having been convinced that the woman's rightful role was to enhance the positions of others, many women simply become immobilized at the prospect of taking a risk.

Explanation 2: "I've got too much to lose. I've worked hard to get where I am and I'm not going to put it on the line. You know what they say, 'a bird in the hand is worth two in the bush.'"

Hennig and Jardin point out that men and women seem to differ on another dimension of risk. Men see risk as affecting the future, whether positively or negatively. Women, on the other hand, tend to see risk as only affecting the here and now. We usually have an eye less on what's to come than on maintaining what we've already achieved. Again this isn't surprising, considering that most of us are aware of society's ambivalence toward our ambitions and aspirations in the work world. No wonder we stand like well-armored guards around our positions and achievements. Nevertheless, that well-planted stance can contribute to keeping us stuck in one place.

Explanation 3: "I've become aware of a game I play with myself. I set my standards so high that I can't possibly meet them — and therefore I don't even try. What it boils down to, I guess, is that I'd rather say I failed because I didn't try than admit I tried and just couldn't do it."

The fear of failure is so powerful it can lead you to deny yourself tremendously valuable opportunities for personal and professional growth. How many times have you turned down the chance to speak or perform in front of people? Or to take part in a new activity, task or game? Or to offer your opinion, ask a question or try out a new idea? All these situations imply a risk — and if you're not willing to be wrong you'll never experience the exhilaration of being right.

If you were asked what the chances are of living your life without making mistakes, you'd probably say close to zero; after all, nobody's perfect. We all know that's the right answer — the trick is in believing it.

Unfortunately, the belief in the right to make a mistake often exists from the neck up. Out of your mouth may come the words "to err is human," yet in your stomach you are struck with the sharp pain of realization that you have just made a mistake. The humiliation, embarrassment and indignation you experience is an indication that, somewhere inside, you believe this mistake had no right to occur. The message your feelings send you is that if you keep trying, you should be able to arrive at that super-human plane where you will be beyond human error. You should be able to become perfect.

It sounds pretty ridiculous, doesn't it? And yet it's a pervasive belief, and the cause of a lot of unnecessary anxiety and undeveloped potential. You can hold yourself back from all you're capable of being simply because you refuse to let go of a belief in your own perfectibility.

When you're miserable over a mistake you made, when you find your imperfections intolerable, cheer yourself up by reading biologist Lewis Thomas' "To Err Is Human" in his book *The Medusa and the Snail.* Thomas maintains that humankind is set apart from the rest of creation by our unique ability to make mistakes. "Mistakes," he writes, "are at the very base of human thought, embedded there, feeding the structure like root nodules. If we were not provided with the knack of being wrong, we could never get anything useful done. . . . We are built to make mistakes, coded for error. . . . What is needed, for progress to be made, is the move based on the error." There. Feel better?

Think of a mistake as an occasional step in an undesired direction among so many steps toward your goal. Viewed in this light, mistakes can even be positive. Remember, they are an important aspect of self-education; there's almost always a valuable lesson to be learned from failure. Failure can teach you to respect your limits and to base your self-esteem not only on what you do, but on who you are and what you value. A perfect record is not a statement of your invincibility, but more likely an indication that you simply are not taking enough risks.

Fear of Success

"What seems risky are the changes I could bring about in my life. Though recognition and power seem inviting now, I worry that there are costs I might not want to pay. For one thing, I'm not sure I would get the support from my family I would need."

Ever since 1970, when Matina Horner first began to publish her work on women and achievement, there has been much misunderstanding and controversy about what has become known as the fear-of-success syndrome. During her graduate studies, Horner became interested in why women, under neutral conditions, scored higher than men on the need to achieve, but scored considerably lower than men on tests measuring the desire to achieve under leadership and competitive conditions. The motive to avoid success in the women tested seemed to be linked to how they perceived acceptable feminine behavior. Since successful achievement is viewed as the result of aggressive and competitive behavior, women felt that achieving success was incompatible with their femininity. In other words, the fear of success was actually a fear of being seen as pushy and unfeminine. The women Horner tested also indicated anxiety about the social rejection they anticipated following success. The most common fears included loss of friends, diminished eligibility as a date or marriage partner, or becoming lonely, isolated and unhappy. The result of Horner's study led her to conclude that "unfortunately, in American society, even today, femininity and competitive achievement continue to be viewed as two desirable but mutually exclusive ends."

Horner's research provided a valuable key for many people concerned with finding ways to enable women to rise to positions of leadership. It was enthusiastically embraced by others, however, as justification for the scarcity of women in government, business, industry and the professions. To this second group Horner's research provided evidence that women don't want to succeed —that, in fact, they want to fail. Since the research was done by a woman, even more credibility was given to the contention that women were solely to blame for having not achieved equal status.

The distortion of the research is absurd to anyone who looks at it closely and objectively. Horner's fear-of-success concept is quite different from a will to fail. Her study indicates that women experience two feelings simultaneously: the desire to succeed and the fear of being punished for doing so. In fact, the women with the greatest ability and the strongest desire to achieve were those most likely to express a fear of success. It follows that those women who want and expect to succeed would be most concerned about the consequences. Moreover, other research has indicated that the fear of success does not necessarily get in the way of performance; many women fear success (as do, by the way, many men who deviate from sex-role expectations) and yet manage to be very successful.

Being caught between feelings of wanting success and fearing the consequences has taken quite a toll on women. Some suffer from headaches, tension or ulcers. Others attempt to disguise their success drive by exaggerating nonthreatening behaviors such as excessive smiling, very feminine dress, passive mannerisms or overly protective and nurturing behaviors. Many women choose simply to keep a low profile and avoid visibility.

As Joanna Rohrbaugh says in her book *Women: Psychology's Puzzle,* "No matter what life choices a woman makes, she tends to worry about her femininity. For one woman this may be a mild concern that emerges only fleetingly when a new wrinkle appears or when others disparage her womanhood. For another woman, however, it may be a constant source of anxiety that can make her hide her abilities and minimize her accomplishments in the male-dominated world of work."

Moving Beyond

You probably didn't learn to swim by throwing yourself into a lake, and you probably aren't going to teach yourself to take more risks by abandoning all restraints. Rather than overwhelm yourself, you'll make more progress by gently nudging your boundaries a little at a time. Stretch yourself in any way that lets you know you're exploring new territory, but not so much that the discomfort discourages you.

In *Paths to Power,* Natasha Josefowitz suggests a progressive order to risk taking: Expressing, requesting and refusing. Let's take a closer look.

1. Expressing. Letting others know what you feel and think is a good first step to increasing your risk-taking abilities. It involves being able to offer opinions or describe your feelings to one other person or within a group of people — even when what you feel is different or not what others wanted you to feel or think. By expressing yourself, you are saying "Take note of me. What I think and feel matters and is valuable." But what if you

find your feelings and thoughts aren't accepted by others — that others find them inappropriate? What if you end up feeling ridiculous or embarrassed? Well, that is the negative side of the risk, isn't it? The positive side is that you could also stand to be praised and acknowledged. And more than that, you have affirmed your personal integrity by respecting your right to offer your opinions.

If you'd like to go a little further, practice initiating — being the first to speak up, to offer a new idea or make contact with others. Breaking new ground is a little scarier. It increases the likelihood of standing out and being noticed, for better or worse.

Even riskier is decision-making. Making decisions expresses your willingness to take responsibility, to act on your information, beliefs, and skills. With any decision goes the risk of the consequences — credit or blame — and most decisions are fraught with a mixture of both. But keep in mind what Josefowitz says: "You never make *the* wrong decision, but only *a* wrong decision."

2. Requesting. Asking for what you want and need is at a higher risk level than expressing. It might include demanding, insisting and confronting. Before you can even ask, you need to know yourself what you want. Do your homework and encourage yourself to allow honest answers to the questions: What do I want? What would I like? What are my needs? It's good practice to ask yourself, even if a given situation doesn't provide you with much choice.

Be willing to be clear in asking others. Initiate rather than wait for others to guess. You might need to be persistent, to ask more than once and in more than one way. The likelihood of getting what you want will be increased if you can show others the benefits to them, if you are willing to explore alternative ways to meet your request, and if you are able to negotiate workable compromises.

3. Refusing. Women have been socialized to believe we should be "nice," serve others and be giving. Therefore, saying no, stating objections, setting limits, rejecting and dismissing

tend to feel very risky. But you will never have credibility unless you are able to exercise these behaviors when they are called for. The risk you run when refusing is to incur the displeasure of others. The task is to challenge your need to have everyone's goodwill all the time. If you need to have everyone pleased with you at all times, you will always be in a dependent position, having sold out your personal power in order to buy approval from others.

Expect to Succeed

Here's how: let go of any ideas about yourself that limit your ability to see yourself as successful. Old patterns and behaviors have to do with yesterday. Today you are growing beyond your limitations, fears and insecurities.

Start sending yourself positive messages. Remind yourself of your accomplishments, strengths, competencies and abilities. Make a list of all the things you do well, and add to that list regularly. Develop a store of positive feelings about yourself that will help you know you have whatever it takes to succeed.

Find the successes in whatever you do, no matter how trivial you think them to be. Always look for the growth you are making — it will be there if you let yourself see it. When you become convinced that growth is happening, you can learn to relax and trust in your own steady progress.

You can turn your emotions into motivators instead of inhibitors. Try relabeling what you feel. The queasy stomach, rapid breathing and tense neck muscles that you used to call anxiety can now be called excitement. Instead of telling yourself you feel pressured, tell yourself you feel challenged. Which makes you more likely to anticipate success — feeling anxious or feeling excited, feeling pressured or feeling challenged? Labels carry forecasts, so forecast success for yourself.

Imagination is a powerful tool you can use to defeat self-doubt. Before you tackle that new assignment, ask for that raise, face that panel of interviewers, imagine yourself as you would like to be. Create a mental image of yourself feeling confident, powerful and contented. See yourself relaxed and expressive and hear yourself easily presenting clear, convincing ideas. If you visualize yourself as someone who succeeds, you will start to know yourself as someone who succeeds.

You can help yourself get started by making a list of five challenges you would like to take on. As you make this list, focus on specific things you're excited about. No doubt there will be anxieties mixed in too, so it's essential to be motivated by real desires to help you push through those insecurities. Allow your list of challenges to be diversified. Anything goes, from "I would like to speak to Mary about the conflict between us" to "I would like to start my own business."

Now, rewrite all five challenges, using the words "I will" instead of "I would like to."

What a difference two words can make! "I will" is the language of a personally powerful woman, of someone who believes in herself and expects herself to succeed. When you say "I will" you are writing yourself a script for success — a self-fulfilling prophecy. Challenges are taken out of the category of "maybe-someday" wishes and placed in the category of "starting-now" plans. Heed the advice of Clementine Paddleford: "Never grow a wishbone, daughter, where your backbone ought to be."

PACT: A Goal Achievement Strategy

After you have set your "I will" goal, try the "PACT" approach to implementing it. PACT focuses your thoughts on calculating the payoffs and costs of your risks, and on organizing a step-by-step approach that will increase the likelihood of success.

Pinpoint

The first step in PACT is to specify your goal. Go over your goal until you are sure it is stated in the most specific terms possible. For example, "to get my writing published" is too general; more specific would be "to get an article on alcohol abuse published in a professional journal." One reason people don't accomplish their goals is because they keep them so general they can never get a firm enough grip on them, and therefore, can't focus on the necessary steps to take.

Now pinpoint when you will meet this goal. Yes, that means giving yourself a deadline. Goals without concrete plans for implementation are just dreams; they dissipate unless you nail them down to a time frame. Granted, there are some people for whom deadlines have a negative effect — instead of swinging into action, they freeze up — but that's not true for most of us. So be honest with yourself; unless you are sure a deadline will inhibit you, put down a date.

If you end up having to give yourself more time, that's all right — at least you now have a target to aim for.

Action

The second step in PACT is action. Break down your main goal into its smaller components. A step-by-step approach helps you make your goal more manageable and keeps you from being overwhelmed or discouraged. For example, our goal of getting an article on alcohol abuse published in a professional journal can be broken down into these subgoals:

- Read professional journals to see style and content being published
- Brainstorm ideas for article and run them by some helpful people (specify who)
- Make rough outline for the article
- Gather and read references
- Revise outline
- Write the first section
- Write the second section; and so on.

Of course, each of these subgoals has its own time frame, the purpose of which is not to make you feel anxious, but to keep you focused, organized and moving ahead.

Consequences

The third step is reckoning the consequences of your actions. Now that you know you can manage your goal, get clear on what the payoffs and costs might be. It's like keeping a ledger in which you tally up the debits against the credits. This step helps you make sure whether you really want to follow through on a particular plan. The more clearly you can formulate a picture in your mind of how you stand to benefit, the more motivated you're likely to feel to take action. At the same time, let yourself be aware from the beginning what you might have to give up to accomplish your goals. This will help you assess if it's really worth it — and also keep you from losing heart later on due to unanticipated costs. Examples of some of the benefits of getting your article published might be:

- Gaining recognition by other professionals
- Feeling pride at having contributed to the field

Possible costs include:

- Having less time to spend with family and friends
- Having to face the possibility of rejections from publishers

List all the benefits and costs you can think of that may result from pursuing and achieving your goal

Track

After you have started on your way stop and check your PACT occasionally to see if you're on schedule and following through in the way outlined. If you aren't, the important question is, why not? Reevaluate your plan and revise it if necessary. After all, the purpose of the plan is to help you accomplish your goals — if it's not doing that, find out why. Maybe you're lacking in resources; figure out what they are and make getting them part of your action step. Maybe your time schedule was unrealistic; give yourself more time if you need it.

We frequently hear people say they can't afford to take risks. But the professional and business woman striving for recognition and increased personal power can't afford not to. As you encourage and educate yourself on the art of risk taking, keep in mind the advice of David Lloyd George, "Don't be afraid to take a big step if one is indicated. You can't cross a chasm in two small jumps."

4. Women and Money

I grew up with mixed expectations about women and money. I never doubted that women were capable of managing finances because for twenty-five years I had seen my mother work as head bookkeeper in my father's business. She took primary responsibility for the business's financial accounting as well as for hiring and training personnel to work under her. My mother also took charge of the family's finances, doing the taxes, managing savings, seeking investments, paying the monthly bills. In fact, she once said that since she had been signing my father's signature on checks for years she doubted that the bank would cash a check my father had signed himself.

But I also grew up seeing that women rarely sought financial independence. After all, it was legally my father's business, it was his name my mother signed, and for most of the twenty-five years she worked, my mother drew only a token salary. Helping my father was her main motivation for working, she said.

When I was ten, I saw the school principal hand my fourth grade teacher her paycheck. Surprised, I blurted out, "Mrs. Pacelli, you get paid for this?" The look on her face showed she was deciding whether or not to be insulted.

"Of course," she said, "Did you think I worked for nothing?" Actually, I did. Teachers worked because they were dedicated — not for money!

Even when I took my first full-time job after college, I unconsciously carried with me the attitude that women weren't supposed to care too much about being paid for their labor. I was a bit surprised and grateful every time I received a paycheck; deep within me was still the childlike belief that no one really had to pay me for my work. But I quickly began to discover that having my own money made me feel free and having someone pay me for my work made me feel important. I still associate earning my own money with having choices and independence, but most importantly, with being valued.

— AL

Spring, 1978. It's a glorious day. I'm on my way to the bank to purchase a loan for a lovely two-family home — my first house! It's a wonderful feeling, but the decision-making process has been long and difficult. Did I want the responsibility? Could I handle it alone? Did the home repair course at the neighborhood center really prepare me to own a home and be a landlady? I was going against an ingrained stereotype that stated women don't buy houses alone, they wait until they are married — and defying a stereotype requires a certain courage.

All of these concerns triggered my anxiety, but my greatest fears centered around the financial commitment. I had never trusted myself to pay on anything greater than a gas credit card (you can't buy more gas than you need!), and so a house was quite a mental and financial leap for me. It meant dealing with banks and lawyers and having credit checks and my life scrutinized.

I was raised to never owe anyone anything in order to ensure my independence, but I also observed my family buying property because "land was the only investment that can be trusted." My challenge was to integrate these two messages in my own mind and find a way past my fears.

The help I needed came from a dear friend, Mark. He was raised to believe that money was to be used and not feared. He even offered to lend me money for the down payment. Although this scared me more on one hand because I now would owe the bank and a friend (the myth if you borrow money in a friendship it ruins it) it ultimately gave me the encouragement I needed to move ahead. I applied for the mortgage and was accepted. My only moment of true panic came when I got the closing statement — where had they found all those hidden costs?!

In the process of buying my house I learned a great deal, but my most startling realization was that for me money was a key to so many less tangible values; most important, trust, confidence, and the belief that I could honor a long-term commitment without fear.

— DAL

Money is this culture's yardstick, our society's reward for valued service. Money buys food, clothing and shelter, as well as the luxuries of the good life. Not having money often causes feelings of hopelessness, helplessness and despair.

In our society a product's price is the visible, tangible representation of its value or worth. From the individual to the international level, priorities are communicated through the withholding or bestowing of money. Some people spend their entire lives obsessed with making, saving, investing and spending it; others avoid it as if it carried the plague. Wherever you place yourself on this continuum, it's absolutely mandatory as a professional woman to understand your relationship with money.

Betty Harragan, author of *Games Mother Never Taught You,* calls money the scorecard in the competitive game of business. She further states that it would take an entire book to untangle the subconscious fears and incredible fantasies that the single noun *money* evokes for most women. In this chapter we will view some of the historical, cultural and psychological myths and realities that contribute to women's attitudes about money, then outline a plan for removing the roadblocks.

Fears

Many women are afraid that if they are too successful they will be left alone; that, by rejecting the traditional woman's role, they will sacrifice the security of a loving relationship, as well as other rewards. Other fears center around the ability to deal successfully with financial matters. How many times have you heard a woman say "Oh, I just don't have a head for figures?" She has probably accepted the negative stereotype that men are better at quantitative and abstract thinking, while women are more successful with verbal skills. This is a major roadblock to attaining positions of power, since many of these positions demand ease with numbers.

Fears associated with money are a natural result of the traditional woman's role, in which a woman either wasn't employed at all or was paid considerably less than her male partner. The woman of the house was often given a fairly tight budget on which to meet the needs of her family, or an allowance for incidentals after her husband handled the monthly bills. Neither situation provides much experience in managing and investing money. The fears associated with this system were exacerbated by divorce, separation or the husband's death. In these cases, the woman of the house becomes responsible for money matters — usually for the first time in her life. No wonder she is thrown into a state of panic.

Betty Friedan gives an interesting perspective on women in this dilemma. She states in *The Second Stage*, "Economic reality cuts across both feminine and feminist mystiques. The fear of ending up like women they all know, who looked to marriage for security and ended up alone and desperate, has forced a lot of women today, married or not, to look for security in their careers."

That's not a bad idea.

Myths

Religious myths that reinforce the glory of the poor and the "true" poverty of the rich have also discouraged women from breaking out of the traditional mold. In her book *Prospering Woman,* Ruth Ross, a California-based psychologist, urges women to come to terms with their fears and reservations about money and to switch from a poverty mentality ("I don't deserve; I'm not worthy") to a prosperity mentality ("I deserve; I am worthy"). She points out that many of the reservations that block prosperity come from beliefs based on misconstrued Biblical sayings. For example, "Blessed are the poor in spirit, for theirs is the Kingdom of Heaven" has frequently been quoted to condemn wealth and praise poverty, she explains. With better understanding of the old translations, however, new interpretation among Biblical scholars shows that the original intention of this and other passages was positive. We now know *poor* originally meant humble and receptive, not poverty-stricken.

Other Bible passages, such as "It is easier for a camel to fit through the eye of a needle than for a rich man to enter the Kingdom of Heaven" have been used to assert that being wealthy is morally wrong. According to modern-day schools, this passage originally referred, not to wealth itself, but to the difficulties inherent when we are controlled by our possessions rather than being in control of them.

Fantasies

When a woman dreams of a life where money flows freely, imagining travel, clothes, jewels, elaborate homes, cars and status, a powerful, wealthy man is usually part of the fantasy. It is this Prince Charming who is the source of life's finer things. He will take care of her forever, so the fantasy goes, allowing her to pursue varying levels of self-actualization. Seldom does a woman dream of money independent of a male source; seldom does a woman dream of owning the status and power, with its resultant independence and control, that this kind of money affords.

It is our firm position that in order to be financially victorious in the political and professional arena we must first learn to be financially victorious in our own minds! Therefore, it is necessary to get some historical perspective on this issue. Often, by tracing the cultural development of a problem, we can release ourselves from feelings of individual powerlessness. When we become aware of the origins of a damaging stereotype or attitude, we often realize that prior constraints are not necessarily present-day handicaps. On the contrary, we can make those very processes work for us rather than against us.

Historical Perspective

Because women's development in the money arena varies from men's, the first place to explore is the historical role relationship between the sexes. In hunting and gathering societies, both sexes were dependent on clear boundaries for men and women. Women traded their ability to forage, care for children and maintain the home in exchange for the protection and fresh game the hunter provided. In *The Clan of the Cave Bear,* Jean M. Auel illustrates a fictitious primitive society in which strict social order and custom demanded absolute division of labor and responsibilities between sexes. Crossing sex-role boundaries was punishable by ostracism and sometimes death. Group life depended on both sexes maintaining the delicate balance that had determined their surivival for centuries. As the novel develops, Ayla, a young woman from a different culture who lives with the clan, crosses one of the sex-role boundaries by expressing her desire to hunt — a strictly male activity. After being banished from the tribe for acting on this desire, a fate expected by the group to result in death, she kills her first wild animal and rejoices in her own primitive power. She realizes that by this single act she has reversed her fate. She will live, because she can take care of herself. Ironically, the very activity that caused her to be ostracized is also the skill that will ensure her survival. Today, long removed from the cave, we can see this story as a metaphor for a modern-day priority: economic survival.

Our present-day social and economic systems got their start in the late eighteenth century, with the Industrial Revolution. Millions of people left family-based occupations on farms and in small towns to work in mills and factories in the city. As Alvin Toffler relates in *The Third Wave,* this resulted in the separation of the production and consumption of goods. No longer did the majority of people live off food they grew or items they made. The middle person and the concept of *doing business* were born. Money became more important in enabling people to satisfy their basic needs. In addition to the creation of "product" and "consumer," there came yet another separation — that between the sexes. A double standard developed. The man was paid directly in currency for his work; the woman was "paid" with food, shelter and clothing for herself and her children.

Ian Watt, in his book *The Rise of the Novel,* further describes the woman's position in society during the Industrial Revolution. He relates that women were totally dependent on marriage for economic survival; a woman's wage in the late eighteenth century was approximately a quarter of a man's, and her property automatically became her husband's upon marriage. In this economic system, virtue was a commodity to be sold to the highest bidder. Virginity relinquished before marriage inevitably meant that a woman was less marketable and therefore less likely to survive economically. It is interesting to note that historically the double standard for male and female sexual activity was reinforced, not only by religious, but also by economic influences. As the culture developed along these lines, we see the polarization of economic roles paralleled by polarization of psychological roles:

Men — independent financially/women — dependent financially;

Men — independent psychologically/women — dependent psychologically.

Independence and Money

A sense of self-reliance, confidence and personal power is derived in part from our belief that we can take care of ourselves — that we can assure our own survival. In today's culture we continue to be challenged by the hunt. Although we are no longer expected to kill wild game, we are expected to trade skills and resources for money to purchase the things necessary for survival and enrichment. Our sense of accomplishment depends on how well we manage the hunt.

The difficulties and opportunities of the modern woman center around the fact that we have no clearly defined role to follow. Women's roles in today's culture have dramatically changed and are fraught with ambiguity. Statistics give undeniable evidence that the American work place is in the midst of a great cultural transition. Whether for personal, social, psychological or economic reasons, women are entering the work force at an unprecedented rate. Of American workers, 42 percent are female. Of these, 41 percent have children under three years of age, and many are single or divorced. Though the number of working women has significantly increased, there continues to be a disturbing disparity between women's and men's salaries: Today's woman earns fifty-nine cents for every dollar earned by a man.

The American work place will continue to change, and every woman can influence change in a favorable direction by adopting strategies to bring her greater economic equality. A psychological strategy is to adopt "as if" behavior. Though you may be inexperienced and anxious about money matters, though you may be expected to accept less than your fair share financially because you are a woman, you can act "as if" none of this were true. As many disabled people will attest, when you act as if a handicap were not real, you challenge yourself to find ways to be free from the constraints of the handicap. Other people pick up on this attitude, and tend to accept you as you present yourself to be.

You can begin to free yourself from the constraints of economic inequality by being conscious of the skills, resources and commitment you bring to your job, and by acting "as if" you expect appropriate financial exchange — in other words, by directly asking for fair pay. Whenever budgets are being slashed and cutback is the name of the game (as has been our experience the past few years), confident requests for financial reimbursement require courage. In fact it becomes all the more important to assert your right to fair reimbursement for your skills and abilities. Even if initially you do not get what you ask for, you have made your expectations clear. If you persist, and are willing to negotiate and collaborate, you can see yourself through the difficult times and set the stage for future success.

Be creative! If money is tight, what other benefits can be traded for your services? A company car, increased insurance benefits, a greater option to buy company stock, a more pleasant working space? The question to yourself should be, "How can I add to the quality of my personal and professional life during this time of economic strain?" Above all, nurture your belief that you *do deserve,* and act as if you expect fair compensation.

Women must challenge the stereotype that we have no aptitude for financial matters. This belief is introduced in early girlhood and reinforced throughout adulthood, resulting in the financial dependence of many women. Even those who are financially independent frequently remain naive enough about money matters to seriously limit their financial and professional success. A recent interview with a multimillion dollar investment lawyer typifies a common stereotypical belief:

Question: Do you experience differences in the way men and women negotiate the financial deals you are involved with?

Lawyer: You're not going to like this, but I've *never* done a major financial deal where a woman was even involved.

Question: Not one? Not even where she was a partner or member of the other team?

Lawyer: There was one, but she was a very minor partner, took notes and never talked. But then, women don't really have an aptitude for money. That begins early, when they don't do well in math in grade school.

One-third the MBA candidates today are women and this is worth applauding. But until women in other professions learn the language of money, the meaning of negotiating and dealing in the area of financial risk, we will continue to be denied true power, both economically and politically.

For example, one place where women have been hurt from inexperience with money has been on the political battleground. Listen to the words of Democratic Congresswoman Geraldine Ferraro: "I still get less in contributions from labor political action committees (PACs) than my male counterparts, but I have more difficulty asking for money." Pat Schroeder, Colorado congresswoman, also attributes her fund-raising difficulties to her gender. "A candidate's network of friends is a crucial source of money, and women do not have access to the people who give large donations to political campaigns." Given that the campaign for a seat in the Senate costs approximately one million dollars (and in the House, half a million), it's no wonder women are having such a difficult time politically. The disappointing truth is that twenty years ago there were seventeen women in the House and two in the Senate; today there are twenty in the House and two in the Senate. Not much progress to show for two decades of work, is it?

The Beginning

The quality of life now and in the future of our society depends on bringing the female principles of nurturing and life-supporting values to bear in economic and political circles. This new cycle begins with our willingness to explore and adjust our attitudes about money, to become members of the financial community, and to put an end to our naivete and dependence on others in handling money matters.

Financial consultant Laura Buglione, along with her associates at The Ross Group in Boulder, Colorado, developed a holistic approach to financial planning. "We are often led to believe that money is an extension of ourselves," she said, "that it is the 'factor' that determines our successes or failures. For many people, particularly women, just thinking about having to deal with money triggers negative emotional responses. Yet in order to become skillful in dealing with money matters these attitudes and feelings must be explored and confronted. For so long, women have been raised with the idea that they would grow up, get married, have children and someone else would take care of the money matters. For many women this fantasy has become a reality, and, as a rule, no matter how independent and successful they become, they do not deal with money skillfully. The primary goal in working with women is to change their way of thinking and to help them realize that they are capable of learning how to take responsibility for their financial futures. In order to establish a comfortable relationship with money, women must overcome the stigma of it as a fearful and ominous object."

Buglione believes that the following exercise is instrumental in developing money goals through understanding attitudes about money. This exercise is divided into two phases. The first explores attitudes and feelings, and the second is a guide to goal-setting.

Phase 1: Exploring Attitudes

1. Who was responsible for handling the money in your family when you were growing up? What was (is) your relationship with them? What values about money did they communicate to you?

2. What are your positive and negative beliefs about having money? Do you feel that you deserve to have it? What do you have to do to get it?

3. What would it be like for you to have all the money you could ever want? What would you buy? Where would you travel? What organizations would you support? How would your life change?

4. Do you feel that you are capable of understanding and learning how to handle money more successfully? If yes, what's stopping you? If no, why not?

5. Do you believe that money brings you happiness? What does money mean to you? What does not having money mean to you?

6. What amount of money would you be comfortable having? What is a lot of money for you?

7. What is your definition of money?

Our friend Susan, after going through the above questions, discovered that her feelings were very tied to her father's attitude and behavior about money and hard work. He owned a small clothing store in a large suburb in the Northeast. She saw her father struggle continually to meet payments, work twelve- to fourteen-hour days, take only infrequent vacations which he did not enjoy, and ultimately die of a heart attack at fifty-two. She realizes now that her caution and negative attitude about money is the result of a decision she made early in life from watching her father. She felt that if she never got too close to money, didn't buy much and lived sparingly, she could be saved from the stress and unforgiving nature of a monied existence. For Susan, denying what she wanted was to be the path of freedom from money's evils. Instead of freedom, she got a hard life with few comforts, little travel, no luxuries, and an impoverished outlook. She failed to realize that money itself is not inherently good or evil. Money did not kill her father, and the pressures of her father's life won't necessarily recur in hers if she begins to consciously integrate money into her lifestyle. In fact, Susan has benefited from her father's experience, for she can make conscious choices to do things differently based on her self-realization and awareness.

Another friend, Donna, who spent a great deal of time over the last couple of years thinking through her present attitude and behavior about money, has discovered that she also is still reacting to early family experiences. Donna's father worked full time to support himself, his wife and several children. Although her mother managed the home and children, she did so on virtually no money, because Donna's father took responsibility for all of the family's financial needs (including food shopping!). If the children ever wanted anything, they had to prove the logic and worthiness of the request to their father or they would be turned down. Donna's mother, who often empathized with the children, could wield little influence because she herself had to go through the same process for justification.

Donna came out of this situation determined *never* to be financially dependent on anyone, and never to have to justify her wants to another person. Her total financial independence worked fine until she married at thirty and had to pool some of her resources with her husband in order to realize their common goals. Although she wanted to make collaborative decisions and share resources, her underlying fear was that she was sacrificing her independence. The beginning of Donna's ability to work through this inner conflict came with the realization that her attitudes were greatly influenced by her early family experiences.

The struggle with dependence, interdependence and independence confronts every partnership — consciously or unconsciously — and most frequently gets worked through in the financial area. In a relationship, money can become the tangible manifestation of less substantive dynamics. To some couples, money represents who gives, who takes, how much and how often. Money can be the battleground for working through issues that are much more complex than actual dollars and cents; for example, issues of how love, affection, anger, control and power are shared. For this reason, awareness of your attitudes toward money — what they are and where they come from — can increase your awareness of many other parts of your life. Attitudes toward power and control in your relationships with others may be clarified by an increased awareness of the ways you relate to money, and your awareness will increase dramatically if you take time to think through the money attitude questions at the beginning of this section.

Phase 2: Goal Setting

Paula Nelson, author of *The Joy of Money,* interviewed Carol Sapin Gold, who owns a very successful communications and personnel relations training firm. When asked "What do you consider the key element to your business success?" Carol responded: "I'm a goal setter. I establish goals to separate the wheat from the chaff, so I can zero in on what I really want. Once I set a goal for myself, I visualize myself doing it, and then I can go back and work out how to get there on a step-to-step basis. Then I go into immediate action. It isn't an overnight process. Goals create energy, because suddenly your energy can be directed in one channel instead of flowing in twenty undefined directions. I've *never* met a successful person who doesn't set and use goals!"

Charles L. Hughes, in his book *Goal Setting,* gives a profile of the individual who sets goals. This person exhibits confidence, is action-minded, and expects to win. This person feels a strong need to tackle tough goals and achieve them, not just well, but with excellence. He or she sets short- and long-term goals and plans ahead. The goal setter believes that people make their own luck, and therefore takes a great deal of individual responsibility and concern for goals. The person Hughes describes takes active control over his or her life. The belief in being able to create one's own reality — to act on one's world rather than being acted upon — is the very foundation of the goal-setting process.

The essence of this action is assertively going after what you want, not waiting patiently for someone to do it for you or to you. The core of being proactive, as opposed to reactive, is belief in yourself and your ability to persevere. A colleague who owns a successful management training firm said that the single most important ingredient of success for him was persistence, the nuts-and-bolts hard-driving willingness to go after a goal again and again; to concentrate, act and learn from his actions, gaining further information about how to win. In the mind of this type of person, failure to achieve a goal leads to creatively reassessing the steps to get there in the next attempt. Mistakes become the teacher to insure future successes; even failure becomes a tool.

Investment expert Michael Lawrence describes twenty youthful millionaires (under forty) as people who didn't graduate first in their class, didn't receive Rhodes scholarships, and didn't get their Ph.D.s at twenty-three. As a matter of fact, he claims, they are not terribly intelligent or well-educated. They do have one thing in common: psychological self-mastery. These are all people who know who they are, where they have been, where they are going and how they intend to get there. They have an instinctive appreciation for the dual nature of knowledge — the things they know and the things they don't know but can find out. Lawrence goes on to state that to achieve financial success you must appreciate your strengths, know your weaknesses, and mercilessly throttle the temptation to lie to yourself. Self-delusion has the nasty habit of turning into self-destruction.

The following exercise begins with imagination, and moves to planning, acting and evaluating. Start big in order to give your creativity a chance to run wild and then turn to specifics as a way to bring your goal into reality. As you go along, keep in mind that your goals are promises to yourself. You wouldn't want a friend to break a promise to you; don't break a promise to yourself by setting a goal that you don't intend to keep.

As you gradually focus on and accomplish specific goals, you will establish a track record of trust in yourself that will support further success. Allow your imagination and creativity to emerge.

Step 1. Imagine you have an unlimited supply of money available to you — all the money you ever wanted. What do you want to do with it? Allow your imagination to come up with at least five ways you would use your money. (If you skip this question, then you are suffering from the escapist mentality that many of us hang onto when asked to get concrete and specific about money!) Be creative, let your imagination take you on new and untraveled paths.

Step 2. Now, from your list of several options, choose to set as your beginning goals those that can be accomplished in six months to a year, then one to three years, and finally three to five years. Remember, money comes with goals. Without goals, if you make money you will spend it before you even know you have it.

Step 3. Begin with those items on the first list.Take one at a time and focus on making each real. See, feel, taste, smell and hear yourself achieving a goal — turn fantasy into reality by focusing your imagination on the details of the goal you want to achieve. For example, when two women friends originated the Kids' Warehouse, a mail-order business for children's clothing, they began by dividing their major goal into more manageable components. Each step of the way was carefully outlined: determining the merchandise, finding suppliers, designing and distributing advertising, developing a mailing list and securing a bank loan. Each step became a mini-goal in itself. The steps necessary to achieve each mini-goal became the blueprint for immediate action. Remember, money is only a medium of exchange, and if your goal is clear, then your sense of purpose and determination will help you to channel your energy and resources to attain what you want. Imagination and follow-through can't be overstated — it's absolutely critical to allow yourself to imagine, to wonder, to muse about the way you would use your money and then go into great detail in your planning. Don't remain fixed in old programs or scripts that trigger fear and limitation where money is concerned. If you associate money with evil, think immediately of the positive, useful way you would use *your* money. Goals can help put debilitating attitudes in their place — out of your mind and out of your way!

Step 4. As you work with each goal, be clear about its probable costs and benefits. If you are aware of potential problems, you can prepare for them so they won't surface to catch you off guard. A friend of ours who is studying to be a photographer cut her work schedule to four days a week in order to devote more time to her goal of practicing photography. Having to sacrifice a fifth of her earnings presents difficulties in short-term financial management, but she's convinced the extra practice time will pay off for her in the long run. The pride she is experiencing in her ability to control her time, energy and budget has made her all the more committed to the new arrangement.

Step 5. After you've clearly established your money goals, review them daily. Put them on an index card that you can carry with you at all times. Dr. Marshall Reddick, who conducts seminars on goal setting and real estate, and is coauthor of *Successful Marketing for the Small Business,* carries his card in his jacket pocket at all times. People are sometimes amused by its tattered edges, but they reconsider when they learn he achieved his goal to earn a million dollars in real estate in less than two years by focusing on that little card daily!

Of course, reading your card daily won't be enough. You will have to take action. As economist Peter Drucker states in Paula Nelson's *The Joy of Money:* "The future will not just happen if one wishes hard enough. It requires decision — now. It imposes risk — now. It requires action — now." Do it! If you make your goals your priorities, you will begin the strategies necessary to implement them.

In order to have money to realize your goals, you have to be in the business of making, saving and investing it. In *Real World 101,* Jimmy Calano and Jeff Salzman have outlined a fairly simple and realistic system to assure you the funds to invest in the area of your choice. The plan includes the following advice:

1. Fact: Net income (your income after taxes) is the raw material of wealth. If you spend it, it's gone; if you save and invest it successfully, it becomes wealth.

2. SAVE, SAVE, SAVE: This reminds us of an old saying: "Spend one dollar less than you make and your life will be a joy. Spend a dollar more and it will be a struggle." Calano and Salzman recommend a simple, one-stroke safeguard: Put aside 10 percent of your paycheck (no matter how small) and *don't touch it!* At least not until you have enough to begin investing in the area of your choice.

3. Leverage: Understand and use it. Leverage is a high-risk, high-financial-gain strategy. Here's an example of how it works in real estate.

Let's assume you buy a condo for $40,000, put 10 percent down ($4,000) and mortgage the balance ($36,000) at 15 percent for thirty years. In two years, you sell the condo for the new market value of $52,000. The appreciation will have made you a clean $12,000 profit on your $4,000 investment. That's a 300 percent return on your money.

4. Establish and maintain credit (in your name!). A nurse we recently worked with talked to us of her struggle to establish credit after her divorce. She said she clearly learned one thing: to teach her own daughters the absolute necessity and value of credit in their own name. Banks, utilities, department stores, the phone company, oil companies and major credit cards will all grant you credit if you can prove yourself a worthy customer. Begin with the necessities like utilities and phone and go on to department stores, oil companies, VISA, MasterCard, and American Express. After accumulating some or all of these and managing them proficiently for a period of time, you should have an easier time securing major financing for a real-estate purchase. (Note: The Federal Equal Credit Opportunity Act outlaws sexual discrimination in commercial and consumer credit. The Small Business Administration Act prevents the SBA from discriminating against female applicants for business loans.)

Before exploring the various opportunities for investments, it is mandatory that you give yourself a financial education. Experience will surely become the best teacher, but some working knowledge is necessary before you invest your first dime! As you investigate your options, it will probably become fairly clear to you which areas feel most comfortable or natural to you. The opportunities are plentiful. For a good foundation we highly recommend reading *The Joy of Money* by Paula Nelson. She gives lots of information, from how to budget to what different types of investments are available. She explains each in a way that is understandable for those of you who don't consider yourselves financial wizards (at least not yet). Here are some other tips to help you begin:

- Attend any of hundreds of continuing education classes held at local night schools and colleges. Often accountants and lawyers and local business people run these, and it's a good way to network while learning.
- Join with other women and men who are at the beginning level of their money education and make a commitment to teach each other. This can be a time-saver, and will give you some insight into what area of moneymaking most attracts you.
- Use the support system you have established already. Think of your friends and relatives — who's making money and how are they doing it? Don't let money be a taboo conversation topic. Tell them you are in the process of a money education and ask questions, no matter how dumb your inquiries sound to you. When appealed to in this way, most people will enjoy giving you the benefit of their learning.
- Get to know your banker. Establish a relationship with someone at the bank (you might begin with a loan officer) that you can drop in on to ask questions and discuss your financial matters. Be confident. Even though you might be a small-time operator now, act as if you have great plans for yourself, and, if treated nicely, might include your banker in them. Re-

member, banks are in the business of selling money; they are like any other store with which you do business. You are a customer, and that affords you certain rights. Use them in a professional manner to further your financial education.

5. Making Presentations

In the ten years I have been training large groups of people, I've had to learn one critical skill of effective speaking on my own — that is, to find and make use of the strengths of my own personality. People could and did teach me the techniques of designing, preparing, practicing and presenting, but the art of making a presentation come alive was something I had to discover by knowing and trusting myself.

After one of my first presentations, I was disturbed to receive one participant's evaluation of my workshop. She had written, "Good thoughts, but your style presents some pretty stiff competition for Sominex." Though it was disturbing, it wasn't surprising. I could see in people's faces that they weren't spellbound, and I also knew because I'd had to work so hard to plow through the material. Presenting shouldn't be a painful struggle; it should feel more like an animated conversation.

I asked a colleague what he thought the problem was. He said, "You tend to hide behind your thoughts. You put out some great ideas but you leave them out there all by themselves. You've got to get out there with your ideas — I mean you've got to let people see who you are. They will be bored if you don't use your personality to make the material come alive." At first I was defensive. "It sounds as if you are telling me to put on a show. I'm not an entertainer, I'm an educator." He said, 'Arleen, if you're an educator, you've got to be an entertainer.

I've discovered how right he was. I couldn't just demand attention; I had to inspire people to want to offer it. Fortunately, it didn't take a five piece brass band to accomplish this. What it did take was discovering the most engaging characteristics of my personality and using them in every way possible. Learning which qualities to use came by listening to what people said they enjoyed about me — and by paying attention to when I most enjoyed myself.

People who have observed both Dolores and me present often comment on the many similarities in our techniques, values and styles. If those people watch closely, they also note the differences of our styles — how we each rely on different parts of our personalities. I've learned to use my warmth and humor to help people feel welcomed and relaxed, and therefore they naturally open up to new ideas. Dolores' strength is in her high energy; her spunkiness captivates people's attention and desire to learn. The added payoff for both of us is that public speaking has become fun and an opportunity to enjoy ourselves!

— AL

For me, the major difference between a mediocre and a great presentation is rapport with the participants. When I don't establish a strong rapport, the day feels more like work; I feel less energy and greater fatigue afterwards. I also experience the feeling of frustration that comes with wanting something to happen that doesn't, the feeling of missed opportunity.

Rather than leave it to chance as I've done in the past, I have begun consciously monitoring what I do to establish rapport with participants. My method is to make contact with individuals in the room who appear immediately responsive. I refer frequently to these individuals initially, gradually broadening the number of people I talk to.

I also ask questions and share some examples from my own life early on to build the areas of commonality in our lives. I do some homework beforehand to assess the "costume" of the group

I will be speaking to and dress according to this assessment. I dress very differently for a presentation with a group of lawyers than a workshop at the local university. I do this to increase my own comfort and to fit in with the group I'm working with — this lets me forget about what I have on and concentrate on what I'm saying.

The last step that I'm aware of in establishing rapport with others is preparing myself before I begin, spending whatever time I can spare (a minimum of five minutes) to see how I am, program my attitude and check out my own expectations of the group. It's amazing to me that when I tell myself the presentation will be fun, stimulating and enriching for all of us, it often happens that way. I think the most significant discovery for me is if I'm communicating with and, feel good about myself, it's easier to communicate with others.

— DAL

Making presentations is one of the best ways to build your personal power and professional impact. It gives you visibility in your organization and respect from your peers — the fact is, the person able to communicate an idea is often credited with having had it. If you are afraid of speaking in front of people (the *Book of Lists* ranks public speaking as one of the top ten fears) or don't know how to go about it, now is the time to get started. It will pay off handsomely.

The four steps of public speaking are *prepare, practice, present, process.* You can remember them as the Four P's.

The Preparation Stage

The first challenge in preparation for a presentation is to find enthusiasm for what you are saying. Have you ever wondered why you were ignored at a meeting and your great ideas went unheard? If so, it's possible that your ideas were sound but your delivery was lacking. Dr. Robert Rutherford, a nationally known management trainer, puts it this way: "If you're not going to be enthusiastic about what you are saying, then who is going to be?"

If you believe that a worthwhile message will sell itself, you're wrong! It is your responsibility to use all of your creative resources to invest energy, enthusiasm, conviction and spontaneity into your spoken and unspoken message. That way it will come alive — for you in the preparation and for your audience during the presentation itself.

So if you are presenting in an area that doesn't excite you, or if you don't feel strongly about it, we suggest you do a bit of homework first:

1. Find someone who does have enthusiasm (lots of it) for the topic and talk with that person; pick his or her brain, see the subject through his or her eyes, and you will soon begin to understand its merits.

2. Read about the subject and discuss it with a friend or colleague to tease out the points of interest.

3. If, after trying both of these suggestions, you can't work up some degree of enthusiasm, ask someone else to make the presentation. Otherwise you will end up boring your listeners — unless you are a very good actor.

Next, you need to know the goals of the people who will be listening to you. Why have they asked you to speak to them? How will they benefit from your presentation? If you keep the audience in mind — who they are and what their needs are — throughout the preparation and organization of your topic, you will be more likely to remain on target throughout your talk. A presentation is not one-way communication, it's a dialogue between you and your audience. Joel Weldon, a famous public speaker, says participants should get involved in the first five minutes. As you prepare your speech, work in some of the following techniques for fostering participation.

Ask a rhetorical question, one that stimulates the audience to think about the subject matter, such as, "Have you ever wondered what would happen if. . . ." Or offer some startling fact or statistic to grab their attention and get them emotionally involved: "Twenty years ago there were seventeen women in the House and two in the Senate; today there are twenty in the House and two in the Senate."

Use humor to generate laughter. Laughing is a wonderful way to relax an audience, but if you don't have the timing necessary to tell jokes, *don't*. There are many other ways to facilitate participation that might be more comfortable for you. Nothing is worse than a joke that flops at the beginning of a talk.

If you think it is appropriate, ask the participants to share their expectations and personal goals with you. In addition to getting them involved, this gives you valuable information that you might not have had beforehand.

If the audience consists of fifteen people or less, you might have participants introduce themselves to the whole group. If the audience is large, have people introduce themselves to the people around them. This helps to relax the participants and makes them feel included, which in turn fosters involvement in your presentation.

Add the Color

A talk is boring if a series of facts or thoughts is given with no padding or color to bring them to life. Ellen, a workshop participant, told us of a job interview in which she was asked to describe to interviewers her prior business accomplishments. She told them *what* she did — decrease the number of days her team was absent from work by 27 percent — but did not tell them *how* she did it. The interviewers were left with raw information, and so never quite got a feel for her real talents and skills. Her point was good: she decreased absenteeism by 27 percent. This is one powerful statistic! But, by simply stating this fact with no descriptive or explanatory background material, she as much as gave it away free. One major problem in presentations is the speaker's tendency to fire too much information too quickly, without focusing on information of obvious benefit to the listener. Whether through example, storytelling, metaphor or painting word pictures, your task is to impress upon the listener the significant points you want him or her to remember.

Using our suggestions, Ellen redeveloped her presentation in the following way, describing not only what she did, but also how she did it.

1. Main topic — what she accomplished: decreased absenteeism of team by 27 percent.

2. Secondary topic — how she accomplished it: used different leadership style from the former manager. To change the norms around work behavior, she altered the staff reward system so that workers got privileges for work done well and on time, and for commitment to company goals. Strict limits were set on discussing personal problems, and warnings were given for inappropriate use of time and absenteeism without good cause. Ellen wasn't popular in the beginning, but soon most of the staff members were relieved to be back on track, feeling good about themselves as professionals, and getting positive reinforcement from upper management. Ellen was praised for leading her department to increased professionalism and productivity.

By developing this explanation of her main accomplishment, Ellen was able to tell her interviewers a great deal more about herself than if she had given them a long list of lesser accomplishments. Notice, in this one example, how she demonstrated her skill and ability to: assess a problem accurately; pinpoint a plan of action; implement a plan successfully, aligning her department's behavior with company goals; risk implementing unpopular decisions and setting limits with her staff. All of these factors gave her prospective employers an example of *how* she manages — surely a much more efficient use of her limited interviewing time!

One Person or a Thousand

A successful presenter makes each member of the audience feel like the most important person in the room. It's a good idea to prepare your presentation as if you were planning a dialogue with one other person. This consciousness will keep you tuned into the group on a personal level and remind you that a group is nothing more than a body of individuals. You gain rapport with individuals first and then with the total group.

Visual Aids

If you are planning to use a visual aid, it is critical that you be very familiar with it! Any piece of equipment, be it newsprint, an overhead or fancy charts, can either add to your presentation or turn it into a disaster. Here are some tips from our own experience:

1. *Newsprint and charts.* When using newsprint and a flip-chart, have no more than three or four items written on each piece. If you need more space for the concept you are teaching, then use two newsprints, one on either side of you. This way people won't have to remember what was on the turned page while you are still on the same topic.

If you are using charts, have them professionally done (with newsprint people accept your own handwriting; with reusable charts they expect more). Use color — it will appeal to the right brain of your listeners, activating a more creative, holistic response.

2. *Overhead projector and screen.* Have transparencies professionally printed in color; they can be set in cardboard holders for easy placement and removal. You can write in the margins and use them as valuable memory aids.

Have the projector itself centered directly in front of the screen to ensure a sharp, even image. In one of our workshops, the screen would fit only on an angle in a corner, making the image too large on one side and miniscule on the other — a disaster, and very unprofessional! In such cases, the audience will forget the information, no matter how useful it may be, and focus on the mistake.

Many people choose overhead projectors because the lights can be left on, and both the presenter and the screen are always visible to the audience.

Many libraries and media centers give instruction on the ins and outs of using overhead projectors successfully; it could be worth your while if you are planning to use one.

3. *Slide projector.* The trick with slides is to show each one for fifteen to twenty seconds. Longer runs tend to bore the viewer; shorter runs make the viewer think he or she has missed something. If you need more than twenty seconds for information graphs, budgets or complicated material, for example, or if you are planning a lot of discussion around the information, then forget the slides and use the overhead projector, where the lights are on and you can stay in touch with your audience. A slide show is appropriate only when you think visual images will enhance your subject matter. They should be powerful enough to speak for themselves — so don't detract from their impact by elaborating too much. If you find you have to talk a lot, then maybe you should choose a more effective slide.

A slide show is a big production; you'll need help with lights and set-up. If your total presentation will take a long time, you might want the projector removed after you are through using it. All in all, a slide show is an excellent presentation medium if you can manage the logistics. An assistant is a valuable asset.

Note: with overhead and slide projectors *always* have an extra bulb.

The Practice Stage

The first time you give a presentation should never be the first time. Practice! Go over the actual sequence again and again. Listen to yourself on an audio recorder. If the equipment is available, videotape yourself to monitor your verbal and nonverbal behavior. This kind of feedback is valuable because it uncovers the unconscious mannerism that can sabotage an otherwise good presentation. A coworker of ours had a blind spot while presenting: she never looked at the right front half of a group. When she noticed this during her video session, she tried recalling the people who were seated in the right front row in her last four or five talks, and could not remember one! Her goal, as a result of seeing herself on video, was to begin including the people who sit in the right front of her groups.

If you don't have access to audio or video recording equipment, have friends, coworkers, or your children role play the audience and listen to your presentation.

When practicing, visualize yourself as being calm, yet excited about the opportunity to share with your audience. Imagine them attentive, responsive and willing to participate with you. Pay special attention to your nonverbal behaviors. Be aware of, and ask for feedback on, your eye contact, tone of voice, pacing, gestures, body movements and posture. For detailed advice in this area we suggest Dorothy Sarnoff's excellent book on public speaking, *Make the Most of Your Best*. Following are some suggestions that we have found most helpful in our experience.

Eye Contact

Look directly at your audience, focusing for ten to twenty seconds on each section of people in the room. Scanning the audience too rapidly makes people feel overlooked.

It's a good idea to choose two or three people with whom to maintain eye contact when you need to ground yourself, usually at the beginning of the presentation or when changing the subject.

Singling out one person to address — usually either a particularly supportive or apparently disapproving member of the audience — is a common nervous habit that can spoil the effect of your presentation.

Voice

Good voice tone is critical. People are unconsciously sensitive to sound, and will be uncomfortable if the tone is off. Project your voice by taking adequate breaths and controlling the muscles of your diaphragm. A word of caution: don't strain. If you need more voice projection than you naturally have, use a microphone. Practice will make you comfortable with it, and your audience will appreciate being able to hear you without your having to yell.

Pace your words so you are not speaking too fast or too slowly. About one hundred seventy words per minute is appropriate for the average listener. Too fast frustrates; too slow bores.

If your voice begins to rise, send your thought and awareness down your body to your feet. Your breath will follow your awareness, and you will resume breathing through your diaphragm; this will deepen the tonal quality of your voice. This technique can also be used to control nervousness, by helping you feel more grounded and balanced. Make sure both feet are evenly placed on the floor and wear low heels that give you optimal balance and control. No one has secure footing on four-inch stilettos.

Gestures and Body Movements

Use gestures and movement to add emphasis to those points you want people to remember. Gesture *during* your statement; gesturing before or after looks contrived.

As with all body language, do not raise your hands above your own neckline. It detracts from what you are saying. Other gestures to avoid are pointing, shaking your finger, clenching your fists and crossing your arms; they make you appear angry and closed to group response. When your hands are open and relaxed you look receptive and confident.

Posture

Your posture gives an instant impression to your audience, and continues to influence them throughout your presentation. The best posture is to stand forward with your weight balanced on the balls of your feet. This will give you more energy and flexibility of movement, and you will look as if you are eager and enthusiastic. Do not rock back on your heels, which gives the impression of retreating from your audience.

One of the most useful ways to improve your speaking ability is to use role models, people you really admire and want to emulate. Watch, feel, experience them; take the best of them and add it to the best of you. A colleague once described her experience in emulating a dynamic speaker in this way: "He was so skilled, informative and inspiring that for the next several months when I did a presentation, I pretended I was him. It worked! Now I feel comfortable being me because I have internalized the best of his style and mixed it with mine."

The Presentation Stage

It is the day of your presentation, and whether it is a speech, a planned contribution to a staff meeting, a request for a raise or negotiation of a conflict, you need to center yourself before you actually begin. The goal is to use all of your internal resources to present yourself with personal power and ease.

In order to do this, find and use a statement, image or feeling that captures the powerful you. Nervousness and anxiety are triggered by messages we give ourselves, usually unconsciously. Nervousness increases as we bully ourselves with statements like: "You can't do this," "I'm so nervous I can't wait until this is over," "I'm going to jumble my words," "I'll forget what I have planned to say," "Why would these people listen to me," "Everyone here is brighter and better-looking than I am" — on and on and on down that familiar negative spiral. Nervousness also increases if you respond to a stressful situation with shortness of your breath. In order to give a successful presentation, it is necessary to replace these power-robbing negative statements with positive ones and to consciously monitor your breathing, allowing adequate intake to calm, soothe, and relax yourself. To capture your unique statement, image or feeling, relax and mentally go back to a time when you felt positive, competent, loved, and good about yourself. From this relaxed, confident part of yourself, let a statement emerge that captures all of these positive feelings. Some examples of statements generated by participants in our workshops are:

- I am qualified to present what I know!
- I can do it!
- I am knowledgeable and want to share this with you!
- Stay calm, you are all right!
- I am well-prepared, and you will enjoy listening to me!

Some examples of images and feelings generated by participants are:

- I see a picture of a small cabin in the woods. This image relaxes me because it takes me away from my present uncomfortable situation, giving me a sense of perspective.
- I visualize a balance scale tipping, then quickly equalizing, so that both sides are even. This image usually helps me to regain my own center.
- I feel a kind, strong hand on my shoulder, and a calming force comes over me.

Each individual's centering device is unique. If you don't already have one, take time to discover this valuable resource in yourself.

Now, on to your presentation. If you have prepared yourself and your material and practiced with yourself and in front of others using the techniques mentioned earlier in this chapter, then the actual presentation should run smoothly. The only variable that you usually can't control is your audience. Two types of people in particular, the Challenger and the Talker, call on all the presenter's resources. You can't totally prepare responses, of course, but you *can* plan a general strategy for handling them.

The Challenger is the individual who challenges and questions *frequently.* We have discovered this person to have opinions and statements more often than questions, and he or she usually wants to tell everyone his or her opinion rather than listen to yours. Diplomacy is called for here, and our policy is to treat this individual with firmness, care, respect and acceptance. This means giving such responses as: "You seem to have some experience with what I'm talking about. I would be happy to spend some time after my presentation to talk with you." If he or she jumps in again, and you continue to feel his or her question is a play to get you into a two-way dialogue, firmly restate your initial response — that you would be happy to talk with him or her later. You can also add, "with such a limited amount of time, I need to continue in order to complete my presentation on time." The rest of the audience will appreciate your strategy for several reasons: You set limits using gentle persistence, not putting the person down; you honored the total group's time commitments by assuring them you would do your best to give them the information they came for and get them out on time; and you set a tone for accepting genuine questions and comments, but not ones that would fail to interest the group as a whole.

The Talker distracts the attention of both the presenter and the rest of the audience by chatting to a neighbor during the presentation. Several options are available for dealing with talkers. The one you choose to use will depend on the size, nature and goals of the group. Talkers can be a valuable asset if you want participation, so don't be punitive in dealing with them.

In a very large group where you are giving a standard lecture behind a podium, hope that some assertive individual sitting near the Talkers will request they stop. If you are not committed to standing in one space, moving toward the Talker will surely capture his or her attention and refocus it on you.

A more sophisticated, very useful technique for managing a group is to give a command camouflaged in an anecdote or story. Milton Erickson, the famous hypnotist, perfected this technique to help his therapy clients. To use this technique, issue a command, varying its tone, pace and delivery in some way. Say, for example, you start telling a story in the middle of your sales presentation about the optimum amount consumers would PAY for your product to insure getting the kind of service ATTEN-TION they want. The message is PAY ATTENTION, and your varying delivery of these two words will suggest this to the unconscious mind of your listeners. This technique will take some study and practice, but it is worth the investment of time and energy if you present often.

In a smaller group you can ask the group for comments and see if the talkers volunteer. Depending on the nature of the problem, you might say something like this: "In the past when I have given a presentation on this material, people have gotten so excited they couldn't wait for the break to share their thoughts and feelings. I would appreciate it if you could hold your comments for just a while longer." If more people begin to talk, assume they want to discuss their reactions with you or one another and take the opportunity to use this energy constructively. You might say "Let's take a break in the lecture and have comments and questions from you now. I'm really interested in your viewpoint." Have them talk either directly to you or to each other, afterwards feeding the responses back to you.

In dealing with a "problem" person, it is important to be aware of the feelings of that individual and your need to manage them in a constructive manner. Think to yourself when confronted with such a challenge, "How can I use this person's energy and turn it into a benefit to the group and myself?"

The Processing Stage

After each presentation it is critical to evaluate your performance so that you can learn as much as possible from your experience. For this purpose, the process stage consists of two steps, self-evaluation and feedback. Self-evaluation comes first.

Self-Evaluation

If you get verbal or written feedback at the end of your presentation, save it until after you have had a chance to do your own evaluation. Sidney B. Simon, author of *Negative Criticism*, warns us of a powerful negative phenomenon in this culture. He says we all walk around with red pencils on the end of our fingers, checking off all those things we do wrong and forgetting the things we do right. He suggests the following self-evaluation exercise to look realistically at situations and activities you are involved in so as *not* to end up concentrating on the negative. Answer the questions as thoroughly and honestly as possible after your next presentation.

- What did I do today in my presentation that worked?
- What did I do today in my presentation that did not work? (Be realistic. Don't exaggerate, or blow things out of proportion.)
- If I were to do the same presentation tomorrow, how would I do things differently?

This final question is designed to give you the power of being your own teacher. You *know* what you would do differently, if anything, after any presentation. It is taking the time to ask yourself this critical question that will program the change for your next presentation and turn your mistakes into valuable learning experiences.

Feedback

After you have spent time in your self-evaluation session, move on to getting feedback from others. This can be a special learning tool because of the functional nature of feedback. Feedback is specific, feedback is behaviorally based on observable data, and you can take it or leave it. In other words, you don't have to buy everything your constructive critic is selling. You are the ultimate judge of how useful the information is to you.

With these parameters in mind, the task is to ask your audience questions similar to those you asked in your own self-evaluation:

- What did I do today in my presentation that was most valuable to you?
- What did I do today in my presentation that was least valuable to you?
- If you were to participate in my presentation again tomorrow, what would you like to see changed?

Successful presentations don't just happen. They are not the result of luck or innate talent. Presentation skills are earned by those who prepare, practice, present and evaluate. As in any other skills-based activity, you can be a terminal beginner, a mediocre speaker or a dynamic presenter, depending on the degree to which you invest your time and energy.

6. Criticism

I don't ever expect to be 100% comfortable with hearing criticism, but I know from experience that managing and monitoring it is within my power. For me the key is to first control the critical voice in my own head that can be so ready to pass judgment on my every move. In all fairness, I have to admit that judging voice has often served me well; it has helped me see my accomplishments and grow from my mistakes. But sometimes it goes haywire, loses perspective and needs to be silenced.

A while back when I was job hunting, I spent several days being interviewed for various positions. As I was driving home after each interview, I would think over my conversations and try to analyze how they had gone. My critical voice would be fairly reasonable at the beginning: "Well, that's over. You covered a lot of ground, gave them a good overview of your experience, showed your enthusiasm." Next it would begin to raise questions: "Maybe you should have stressed your writing abilities more. Do you think they got a clear enough idea of your leadership skills? What if they misinterpreted your statement about your values and goals?" Before long my voice was moving out of raising questions and into hurling accusations: "You shouldn't have come across so pleasant and friendly — you make them think you can't be firm and confrontive. You didn't offer one piece of evidence that you understand, much less care, about their long-range goals. Your reply to their last question was totally evasive — and don't think they didn't notice! They can't possibly believe your interests are compatible with theirs after what you said." Eventually the final judgment would be passed: "Well, you certainly blew that one!"

By the time I arrived home my confidence would be shot, and facing the next interview seemed overwhelming. This is not what I needed. If I was to project personal power in the next interview, I would have to stop the self-criticism. I decided my strategy would be to censor my message to myself. The next time the situation arose, I flatly refused to permit the critical voice to speak. Instead, as the destructive criticisms began, I would think, "No! Stop it. You aren't allowed to do this. Think of something positive to say to yourself." I'd repeat that same message to myself as often as needed, until persistence and determination won out. I trained myself to offer encouragement instead of criticism, which in turn proved to me how much more productive people are when the focus is on their strengths. Eventually, I also began to be less vulnerable to much of other people's unhelpful criticism, which was usually much less stinging than my own.

— AL

Criticism always had a tremendous impact on me. When I was criticized as a child the most important thing was to win back the approval of the critic. I would overapologize, overjustify, overexplain and overcompensate to make up for what I had done. I was a critic's perfect prey. Probably the most unfortunate part of my response was the fact that long after the critic had forgotten the event, I was still making up for it because the critic in my own mind had become relentless.

I recall being very cautious with family and friends so as not to incur their displeasure, and I'm now convinced I always took the safe road because I couldn't tolerate the thought of risking judgment by another's (or my own) critical eye.

I was well into graduate school when a professor introduced me to a book that would change the direction of my life. She suggested that I read When I Say No, I Feel Guilty *by Manuel Smith to explore assertiveness, knowing that one of the basic tenets was learning to deal effectively with criticism. The section entitled, "Criticism: The Great Manipulator" was certainly healing for my sore and scattered ego. Throughout was a clear message that I desperately needed to hear — I must take the power back from all those people I had given it to and begin judging my behavior myself, taking both control of and responsibility for my own actions. They were words that I had no reference for, but with Smith's descriptive examples of how criticism is used as a tool by others to control our behavior, I got a clearer idea of how I could begin sorting out useful from destructive, manipulative and nonproductive criticism from others — and more important, from myself!*

—DAL

Criticism hurts. Many of us have an automatic, spontaneous and physical response to being criticised. It can feel as if someone has just pierced us with a sword, and the feeling often lasts long after the critic has delivered his or her statement. Memories of hurtful criticisms from years past can linger, and some we may *never* forget.

Criticism is so powerful because we all have a self-image that we will go to great lengths to defend. Everyone likes to think of himself or herself as a worthwhile person — and everyone defines *worthwhile* according to personal standards and values. Criticism hurts so much because we feel we are being told that we aren't who we thought we were, or who we want to be. Our sense of "OK-ness" is swept away, only to be replaced by self-doubt and insecurity. It's no wonder so many of us spend so much energy avoiding feedback, denying it when we do get it and defending ourselves against its impact.

Fear of criticism can be so strong that some people choose to place themselves only in situations where approval is guaranteed, where they are sure not to displease anyone, or where any kind of feedback is unlikely to come their way. Unfortunately, being only in "safe" situations means avoiding those challenges in life most likely to lead to fulfillment, visibility and recognition.

Women are particularly vulnerable to the fear of criticism because of certain socialization patterns we grew up with. Traditionally, little girls have been raised to believe that their happiness and security depends on the goodwill of others. For a child raised in this belief, pleasing is imperative, because disapproval is a threat to her well-being. As a consequence, most women have grown up to be cautious about the possibility of incurring someone else's displeasure. Many of us have developed the fine art of reading other people's moods and deciphering their subtlest behaviors so we can gear our own behavior to please. In fact, what has been called women's intuition may be just this finely tuned sense of perceiving such environmental clues as gestures, facial expressions, tone of voice and ambiguous verbal messages.

There's no doubt that women today have a greater sense of independence and self-sufficiency. But having only recently gained entrance into male-dominated work spheres, we are ever wary of exclusion. For this reason, criticism often activates feelings of dependence and insecurity.

This need not be, because criticism is actually an important tool of personal power — one you should learn to use. For instance, criticism can help you gain the information you need to move closer to your goals, to be a more effective and included member of your workteam, and to strengthen the relationships that are important to you. There is great value in knowing how you are perceived and how your behavior affects other people. How else can you know if you are having the impact you hope to have, or what changes, if any, you could make to better achieve your goals? Information is power, and having the information about the effects of your behavior empowers you to make the choices that will serve you.

The key to protecting yourself from the unnecessary hurts of criticism and using it to increase your personal power is in learning and practicing effective skills. Remember, if you learned at one point in your life to let criticism have a negative effect on you, you are just as capable of relearning a new response — one that will empower rather than depower you. The first step is to become aware of what your present response to criticism is.

Mismanaging Criticism

In general, there are two major ways you can mismanage criticism: by being overly defensive, and by being self-condemning.

When you are being defensive, you have a tendency to refuse to accept any critical statements. Instead, you deflect them outward, where they can't hurt you, or *externalize.*

Imagine, for example that a coworker confronts you with the following criticism: "Our departments were supposed to present a joint report for the division meeting today. I'm frustrated that you haven't gotten your statistics to me so that we could finish the report by the deadline."

Defensive responses to this criticism might be countercriticizing: "Well, it's no wonder that happened. If you had taken more responsibility to communicate with my department, we could have coordinated our efforts and been on top of things."

Or deflecting responsibility: "Of course, I forgot. You'd forget too if your department was inundated with as much work as mine is. We still haven't received the increase in staff we were promised, you know."

Or denying: "I didn't forget. No one made it clear that those statistics were due by this meeting."

All of these defensive responses have the same theme — "it's not my fault. It's someone or something other than me that's to blame." This behavior is ineffective and often invites resentment. If you rely on these excuses you will be seen as someone who has limited potential because you aren't willing to accept responsibility for your behavior and to learn from your mistakes.

On the other hand, it is equally ineffective to be self-condemning in the face of criticism. The tendency in this case is to unselectively accept all criticisms regardless of the source or the degree of truth. When we blame ourselves indiscriminately we *internalize*. We let in not only every critical statement, but also every negative meaning that can be attached to it.

Consider the following self-condemning responses to the criticism leveled in the previous example.

Over-apologizing: "Oh, I'm so sorry. I can't believe I forgot. I don't know what's the matter with me. You must be furious with me and I don't blame you. I really am sorry."

Over-compensating: "I feel so terrible about this. I hope you can forgive me. I'll see that my staff drops everything and gets as much done on this before the meeting as possible. I'll make a statement at the meeting admitting full blame. And I'll send someone from my department to help you."

Guilt, self-put-downs: "I can't be relied on. Anyone else in my position would have remembered to complete those statistics. Maybe I'm not competent enough for this job. I shouldn't be surprised if I lose the respect of my coworkers because of this. Facing them at the meeting will be humiliating."

The theme underlying an internalizing and self-condemning response to criticism is, "Something is wrong with me. I'm not good enough. I can tell because someone is displeased with me." This undermines your self-confidence and keeps you from acting on your true potential.

Internalizing criticism will cause others to see you as someone who crumbles easily, and though you may gain their sympathy you will lose their respect. Some will resent the need to treat you carefully lest you be wounded or demoralized. Others may pinpoint you as an easy target for scapegoating. Being self-condemning is also inappropriate because someone else's displeasure is not necessarily a measure of your competence, responsibility or worth.

If you are habitually managing criticism in one of these two ways, you have given up your right to choose. The tendency to be defensive or self-condemning is rarely a conscious choice — you do it automatically. Nothing diminishes your personal power more than to abdicate your right to choose. Having personal power means exercising your right to decide which criticisms are worthy of your attention, which can really help you, and how you want to integrate them.

Destructive Criticism

Choosing not to accept and to respond only to certain criticisms may be a very new experience if your social conditioning has taught you to believe that all criticism is good for you. After all, if it hurts, it must be helpful, and the more mature you are, the more criticism you are supposed to be willing to accept, right?

Wrong: *Not* all criticism is good for you. Some is downright destructive, especially if the critic does not really wish you well. The fact is that there are times when people criticize you out of jealousy or malice. Their intention is hardly to give you a tool to help you grow; more likely it is to knock you off balance. Why would you choose to accept such criticism?

Destructive criticism may also come your way when someone is angry with you. It is not unusual for angry feelings to be accompanied by hurtful criticisms, many of which are regretted and retracted later on. Negative criticisms inflicted in the heat of anger are best ignored — they are unreliable and meant more to hurt than to help.

It is always to your benefit to choose not to be affected by criticism that is meant to manipulate you and play unfairly on your emotions. As Manuel Smith says, at times people will attempt to impose their own structure of right and wrong on you. Unfortunately, most of us have been trained to automatically accept the other person's values. For example, a coworker might say to you, "You've been fooling around with that project all day long!" The tone of voice and choice of words imply there is something wrong with your behavior. Often this is an indirect approach to getting you to do what the other person wants (in this case, perhaps, to engage your help elsewhere). But, instead of making a direct request, he or she uses criticism to manipulate you into feeling anxious, stupid or guilty enough to change your behavior. The best way to manage destructive criticism is to gain control of your psychological boundaries. In this way, you choose not to let the criticism hurt, upset or manipulate you. You simply refuse to let it reach you.

Critic: "You've been fooling with that project all day long!"

You: "Yes, it *is* taking quite a while." (Agreeing.)

Critic: "It could have been done three hours ago."

You: "Maybe it *could* have been done sooner." (Agreeing.)

Critic: "You're just not with it today at all, are you?"

You: No response. (Selective ignoring.)

Critic: "Maybe you're not the person for the job."

You: "Do you happen to know if the cafeteria is still open? I could sure use a cup of coffee." (Diverting the criticism.)

Critic: "Everything has come to a standstill because you're not done yet!"

You: (making direct eye contact) "I'm tired and tense. What I need right now is your support, not your criticism." (Directly confronting the criticism.)

Each of your responses keeps your critic's statements at a distance. At no point do you engage in a war of words. Instead, by finding some truth in the statement to agree with, selectively ignoring other statements, changing the subject, and finally directly confronting the process, you maintain your personal power. You give the message, "What you are saying is having little control over me. I will not be upset, angered or manipulated by you."

Answer the following questions as thoughtfully and honestly as you can:

1. Are there certain individuals with whom you habitually fall into "wars of criticism?" Who are they?
2. At what times do you think dealing with criticism effectively and skillfully would be of most help to you?
3. What are the specific benefits of managing your psychological boundaries during these times? What are the costs?
4. What can you silently tell yourself that will remind you of your right and ability to be in control of your psychological boundaries?

Valid Criticism

Now, what about the times when you are criticized because you really have made a mistake? Criticism isn't always manipulative and out of line; sometimes it is appropriate and truly valid. If in fact you have done something that directly hurts, embarrasses, angers, discounts or denies another person, it is reasonable to expect that you will be called on your behavior. Handling valid criticism can often be more painful than invalid criticism, because it reminds you of your fallibility. The more you have invested in seeing yourself as someone who doesn't make mistakes, the more difficult it will be to accept valid criticism.

Accepting yourself when you have erred is the underlying principle of dealing with valid criticism. If you don't accept that you have made mistakes in the past and are likely to make mistakes in the future, then you are forced to live a tightly controlled, low-risk existence, wasting a lot of valuable energy trying to be perfect rather than fully alive.

Denise, not long into her new management position, attended one of our seminars. She described how her fear of making a mistake had been controlling her behavior for the previous two weeks. A few months earlier, when facing her first hiring assignment, she had interviewed several applicants and eventually made a decision. At the time she had felt very confident in her choice, and was sure she had hired a capable person well-suited to the tasks and goals of the organization. However, within a few weeks it became apparent that a mismatch had taken place — not only because the new person lacked the necessary experience, but also because his individual goals were incompatible with those of the organization. Even after having spent significant time and money training him, Denise's superiors and coworkers were relieved when he decided to leave.

His leaving solved one problem for Denise, but left her with another. She was forced to face the fact that she had made the wrong decision in her choice of applicants for the job. She had spent the past two weeks avoiding a confrontation with her superior. When we asked her why she was avoiding her supervisor, she replied, "Because she's going to lay it out to me — tell me I made a big mistake." Well, what was so terrible in hearing that? It wasn't going to be news to her. But, Denise explained, she didn't want to face it squarely. She had been soothing her wounded ego by making excuses for what had happened. She simply found it too painful to admit that she was incompetent to handle the responsibilities of her new position.

Incompetent? As many of us do in similar situations, Denise had made an enormous and unnecessary jump — from realizing she had made a mistake to believing she was incompetent!

Her case is a good example of how we can sabotage our personal power — not by making a mistake, but by assigning more meaning to the mistake than what is realistically called for. Denise's realization that she had hired an unsuitable person shook her self-confidence and self-esteem so much that she wanted to fade into the background. She cast herself as an incompetent, when the truth was that she had merely made a mistake.

When you make your next mistake, activate your personal power to help you respond to your critics. Focus on the present, not the past. In other words, avoid recalling the other times you may have made a similar mistake or been displeased with your behavior. Focusing on the past only provides you with more ammunition to shoot down a positive self-image and interpret your present mistake as proof of your inadequacy.

Instead of engaging in self-punishment, try this: Simply accept responsibility for your behavior. Openly admit that the mistake was yours. Denying, countercriticizing and making excuses won't go over well with other people — or, more important, with yourself. We all know when we are trying to avoid a truth. The sense of integrity that comes when we are congruent on the outside with what we believe on the inside enhances our personal power.

Then, agree with the specifics of the mistakes. This means accepting those parts of the criticism that describe the error and filtering out those statements (whether from you or your critic) that attribute derogatory personality traits to you. For example, accept "You are late for the meeting." Filter out, "You are irresponsible." Focusing on the specifics of the mistake will help you assess if there is anything you can do now about the situation, and can lead you to negotiate a workable compromise.

Let's look at how Denise's inevitable encounter with her superior could be handled with personal power:

Superior: "Denise, I'm really rather concerned about what has happened. Hiring John was a disaster — it cost us several hundreds of dollars in training time, not to mention the disruption in morale and the setback in schedule. I can't believe you could have been so off in your judgment. It's not what I expected from you."

Denise: "You're right. I was way off in my judgment. I realize I overlooked some important variables in assessing John for the job. I'd like to help minimize the negative effects of my mistake." (Agree with specific criticism.)

Superior: "Well, the damage has already been done. What I really want from you are two things: to

Denise: begin the rehiring process immediately, and to assure me this won't ever happen again."

Denise: "I'd be glad to begin rehiring. In fact, there were two strong candidates I'd like to interview again if they're still interested. I don't know if I can promise you this will never happen again. But I do know I've learned from this and will apply what I've learned to future hirings."
(Work toward a compromise and don't respond to guilt.)

The following exercise is designed to help you handle constructive criticism. Answer these questions as thoughtfully and honestly as you can.

1. When is it most difficult for you to accept your mistakes?
2. If fear of making mistakes has been controlling your behavior, what has it cost you?
3. What do you have to gain by being more self-accepting when you err?
4. What can you say to yourself that will encourage your self-acceptance?

There are times when the discomfort of criticism cannot be avoided. Negative criticism has a way of finding you no matter how you try to set up your life and your own behavior to accept it. But it is important to choose not to escape the criticism even if you could, because receiving it could bring a legitimate payoff. Discovering what there is about your behavior that someone else objects to may be the key to a new promotion, a raise or a closer and more rewarding relationship with that person. You might very well find it acceptable, and perhaps even easy, to change when you know specifically what it is that a boss, superior, coworker, or subordinate objects to.

Vague Criticism

But criticism often comes in very vague terms, so that the desired behavior change is hard to pinpoint. For instance, a person is sometimes criticized for having a "bad attitude," and trying to define what that means can result in endless speculation. Does it mean coming late to work, snapping at clients, disagreeing with the boss, or keeping one's desk cluttered? Other common vague criticisms in the work place are "You lack initiative," "You're unprofessional," "You're uncooperative." All have this in common — they don't give enough information to be useful.

An employee cannot be expected to improve an attitude when it's not made clear what is meant by "a good attitude." Nevertheless, job security, raises, promotions, and other rewards might depend on it. Distilling vague criticism into criticism about specific behavior makes it understandable and also removes some of the scariness. For most people it's much less anxiety provoking to hear, "You interrupt too often at staff meetings," than "You're loud and pushy." If criticism is put in terms of behavior rather than personality, and if you see it as someone's objection to your behavior rather than proof of your worthlessness, you have chance of dealing with it effectively.

If someone criticizes you in a vague way, it's up to you to make them clarify their message. Your role is that of an interviewer; you must ask specific questions in a way that conveys your willingness to listen.

Consider the following interchange between Maureen and her boss:

Maureen: "I'm glad you could meet with me, Ms. Y. I'm hoping you can explain to me why I wasn't offered the promotion that was available."

Ms. Y: "The reason you weren't offered the promotion is because you're not ready."

Maureen: "Can you tell me what it is about me that tells you I'm not ready?"

Ms. Y: "Well, you aren't on time with your statistical reports, for one thing."

Maureen: "That's true. I have been late at times. Is there anything else?"

Ms. Y: "You don't seem to be supportive of staff decisions."

Maureen: "In what way do I seem unsupportive of staff decisions?"

Ms. Y: "We decided that the weekly meetings would be chaired on a rotating basis and you haven't volunteered for your turn in quite a while."

Maureen: "So I could be more regular in taking my turn at chairing meetings? Is that right?"

Ms. Y: "Yes, and also in contributing ideas."

Maureen: "It seems I don't contribute enough?"

Ms. Y: "You are very helpful in thinking of ways to activate other people's ideas, but you don't come up with innovative solutions yourself. It makes me wonder if you're thinking hard enough."

Maureen: "So I could try to contribute more creative ideas? Anything else?"

Ms. Y: "No, I think that's it."

Maureen: "Let me see if I've got it all now. I could get my statistical reports in on time, chair meetings when it's my turn, and contribute new ideas at meetings. Is that right?"

Ms. Y: "Yes, that's right."

Maureen: "Thanks for your criticism. It's given me a lot to think about. Could we meet in three to four weeks to discuss it again?"

Ms. Y: "Yes, certainly. And thank you."

What stands out in this example is that Maureen's persistence in asking questions prompted specific information about her behavior. She made a point of not denying the criticism, or becoming defensive or countercritical. Sincerity is important. This same interchange would be a disaster if Maureen accompanied her words with a sneer, hands on her hips, and a challenging tone of voice. Asking for the clarification of vague criticism is not a tool for proving your critics wrong. It is an opportunity to receive information that could be helpful in improving your performance and relationships. Don't ask unless you're ready to hear the answers.

Another way to avoid becoming defensive is to gather information first and deal with it later. You can discuss the criticism in a later conversation with your critic after you've had time to think about what's been said and you're sure you're in control of your feelings. If you have explanations you'd like to offer your critic or if you sincerely disagree with the criticism, you will present your opinions best after you've given yourself time to prepare. Taking some time to think might also make it easier for you to find the truth in what's been said and to think about if and how you'd like to make some changes. A second discussion with your critic might include your requests for his or her help in making the desired changes.

By managing vague criticism in this way you have increased your personal power through:

1. Supplying yourself with specific information that tells you exactly where to direct your efforts should you decide to change.
2. Being in control of your behavior and the expression of your feelings.
3. Presenting yourself as someone who is self-assured enough to be open to other people's opinions, objections, and concerns.
4. Respecting your own need for both specific information and time to deal with it.

Answer the following questions as honestly and thoughtfully as you can.

1. What are some of the vague criticisms you have received and have been unable to work with?
2. Which of your critics have information you would like to receive to help you improve your performance or strengthen your relationship? Ask for it. You don't have to hear from everyone willing to hand you a vague criticism. Exercise your personal power to choose who you really want feedback from.
3. With whom do you feel most comfortable to try this skill first? Be sure to choose someone who is honest, and who respects and likes you.
4. What will be your first question? Remember you can tell your critic when you've had enough. We all have a point at which we become overloaded. Draw the topic to an end before you reach this point.

Turning criticism into a tool to increase your personal power will require patience and persistence. You can do it — and when you do, you will release yourself from the unnecessary fears that block the expression of your full potential. You will be able to listen to whatever is said to you without losing your perspective, temper or self-confidence.

7. Collaboration: The Winning Skill

There is no question that collaborating with Dolores brings out my best. My creativity increases as we hitchhike off each others' ideas. My problem-solving is quicker and better. Even making mistakes is less distressing when she is there to help rectify them. When Dolores and I work together, I like what I produce, and I also like who I am. She has a wonderful way of finding what's "right" in what I do, and through her I have become better able to recognize and appreciate my strengths. She tells me I'm bright, thorough, and articulate, and that she values my caring way of working with people. She also reinforces my sense of humor. When she laughs with me, as she does so often, she is by far my best audience.

My confidence grows and I feel stronger when I collaborate with Dolores. What I doubt I can do myself, I know I can do with her. I take more risks and try new things, partly because I know that even if my efforts flop, she will always find something valuable in what I've done.

I find I am less likely to betray my own values and goals when I work with Dolores. When I get caught up in the moment and lose sight of the meaning of my efforts, Dolores puts me back on track. ("Is this what we really want to be doing? Will this serve us well in the long run? How consistent is this project with our values?")

We have also learned how to integrate each others' personal needs and values into our working style. When my commitments conflict I can count on Dolores to understand and to join me in solving the problem. It is not necessary to justify to her; she accepts.

Working with my dearest friend and my most respected colleague is one of my greatest joys.

— AL

When I began to outline the benefits of collaborating with Arleen, the task seemed overwhelming; the benefits are too numerous and far-reaching. I am convinced this relationship has carried me much further on my career path than I could ever have traveled alone.

I feel my own resources are more than doubled; I take greater risks, confident that between the two of us we can find some resourceful way to follow through in any situation. When I burn out or get so emotionally involved in a situation I don't know which way to turn, Arleen is able to look at the facts and give me some perspective on what's happening. She often comforts by confronting, challenging me to remobilize my strengths.

I also learn a lot from watching her manage people. I'm much more impulsive and aggressive, and sometimes get deadlocked because of this. Arleen moves mountains (and people who are even more rigid) by understanding and listening to them first and then communicating her own needs, desires and concerns. Very effective!

She offers encouragement and support by observing my strengths and weaknesses and pointing them out to me. She thinks when I'm presenting I'm delightful and capable — I often think when working that if no one else responds, Arleen will find something positive about what I've done.

— DAL

In the professional world, teamwork is the name of the game. Look at your own organization: chances are it consists of a number of people, each with different skills, contributing toward a common goal. The idea is for synergy to take effect, making the whole (the productivity of the organization) greater than the sum of its parts (the productivity of all individuals). But synergy will only happen if people work as a team. When people work against each other — and it happens all the time — the whole is much less than the sum of its parts.

Teamwork is not only necessary for organization productivity; it is also necessary for individual fulfillment. Almost everybody likes the feeling of being part of a team, of counting on other people and being able to share the feelings of challenge, victory and, yes, even defeat.

The problem is that many women do not have the lifelong experience of teamwork (unlike boys who grew up with the strong socialization of team sports); and therefore we do not always know *specifically* what is expected of us as team members. As a result we sometimes find ourselves the victims of unhealthy competition, often with the very people with whom we should be working.

Let's define teamwork here as the process of *collaboration.* Morton Deutsch, an organizational consultant famous for his work in analyzing group behavior, defines collaboration and cooperation as "problem-solving and mutual enhancement of the other's power as well as one's own." Therefore collaboration means giving your team members as much information as you can, and communicating by identifying what benefits are available to both parties through cooperation. In other words, the intention in the collaborative process is to show how and what each party is going to win if both parties work together.

Cyril R. Mill and Lawrence C. Porter, both behavioral psychologists, explain that success in the collaborative process demands that stereotypes be dropped and ideas be given consideration on merit, regardless of their source. This requires focusing on the problem at hand and listening for those options that will most successfully handle the situation.

A workshop participant offers the following example. Sally, a member of a team that met to brainstorm ideas for marketing educational materials, recalls that the most innovative ideas often came from, "of all people," Marian, the bookkeeper. She said when Marian first offered ideas everyone would wait quietly until she was through, then pick up where they had left off. After several weeks of politely disregarding her ideas, they discovered that one of her suggestions worked successfully.

The team started to value Marian's input only *after* they had looked beyond the fact that she was the bookkeeper: "We thought she knew only figures and couldn't have creative ideas about anything else." When team members dropped their stereotype of bookkeepers and became open to Marian's suggestions, the group, and ultimately the entire marketing effort, benefited.

Negative and Positive Competition

Deutsch defines the negative competitive process as one which influences through coercion. Threat, punishment and limiting the options of others are the strategies of negative competition. Negative competitors communicate not to clarify an issue, but to mislead others by giving incomplete or false information. Negative competitors are likely to be suspicious and hostile. They focus on how the power, values, and beliefs of others differ from their own. A clear opposition of interest emerges, so that one or both parties come to view the relationship as win/lose: "If I get what I want, then you can't get what you want." When the win/lose attitude determines a team's behavior, the contest usually ends in a win/lose draw. Negative competition can only function successfully for a limited time within an organizational group, for sooner or later the "loser" will get even with the "winner," and all real productivity will cease.

John, an assistant marketing director in a small real estate office that deals in custom-built homes, was a sharp salesman with an excellent record. Mark had been an agent with the company for a little less than six months and was slowly but surely building a clientele. He was hard-driving, aggressive and very determined to succeed. John respected this in Mark and gladly offered him working support. For a while the team was cooperative, and work went well. Then John found out that Mark was not recording or forwarding his messages and as a result John was not able to return calls that could have brought him sales. He also found that often when a customer called, he or she would be told by Mark that John was extremely busy but that he, Mark, would be happy to help.

John was furious. The trust that had been built between him and Mark broke down. Mark, in an effort to set up a win/lose with John, had ultimately set up a lose/lose. No longer was John available to serve as his mentor and sponsor. On the contrary, John now felt betrayed, and so avoided personal contact and withdrew his working support.

This situation exemplifies the deterioration of a team from a win/win (Mark's and John's cooperation in the beginning) to a win/lose (Mark's attempt to gain customers at John's expense) to a lose/lose (John's withdrawal of support and Mark's ensuing isolation in the company).

In the positive competitive process, people match abilities and try to win without malice or dishonesty. This kind of competition is the lifeblood of sportsmanship; its drive fosters progress, new ideas and more creative ways of doing things. Positive competitors seek to outmaneuver their counterparts in the marketplace. Positive competition, on both the individual and the company level, is the challenge that keeps the game of business stimulating and exciting.

A conspicuous example of positive competition today is happening in the computer industry. Each of the companies in this fast-moving industry is competing, not only to offer more and better capabilities, but also the lowest price. Each company has to foster collaboration and synergy among its employees so it can compete effectively in the marketplace. The winner? Everyone: the consumer by getting more for his or her money, the computer companies because they are forced to operate at peak efficiency, and because the increased value of their products industry-wide has broadened the market and increased the pie for all companies.

Male/Female Differences

Let's take a look at some of the differences between typical male and female collaborative and competitive behavioral styles. Sex-role conditioning begins early. Selma Greenberg points out in *Right from the Start: A Non-sexist Approach to Child-Rearing*, "Managing and maintaining control of oneself and managing and maintaining control of others is taught through mastery in individual and team sports — not in dealing with inanimate objects, i.e. dolls, cutouts. Effective strategies for dealing with conflict, confrontation and competition are all absent from dolls and the rest of girls' stereotypic play."

Margaret Hennig and Anne Jardim, in *The Managerial Woman*, go even further: "In childhood and adolescence, in groups and teams, boys support each other, confirming each other's place in a hierarchy of both friendship and dominance and in search of freedom from the structures of authority and adult control. More independent of adult authority, they impose upon themselves a structure of values that includes cooperation and competition."

Boys learn through participation in team sports the all-important rule of doing business: be competent and collaborate with your own team while doing your best to outsmart, outplay and outmaneuver the other team. The better the other team, the more challenging and invigorating the competitive process. Other lessons are also taught by team sports:

1. Do your own job well and count on others to do theirs well! The old saying "If you want something done right, do it yourself" has no place in team sports. In fact, an over-zealous player "going it alone" is seen as a great detriment to a team's potential success.

2. Constructive criticism is the blueprint for success. Not only is it accepted, it is expected. Feedback, strategy sessions, films of the most recent game, all give valuable information about what one is doing wrong so that one can begin doing it right. Criticism is not taken personally; it doesn't make the team player feel unloved, undervalued or untrustworthy. Instead, it is considered a necessary ingredient for making a future winner.

3. Each play fits into a broader strategy designed to achieve the goal: victory. Each play is viewed, not as a solitary event, but as an integral part of the game, influenced by and influencing every other play. Thus the game is a highly orchestrated event, and team members must learn to recognize its complicated interrelationships and play accordingly. This is the basis of strategy. In order to play strategically, the players develop within themselves an impersonal "observer," or "onlooker." Through the eyes of an impersonal observer one's own actions and those of teammates can be watched with a certain degree of detachment, coolly and deliberately assessing what needs to be done as the game progresses. The observer is a mental device which allows one to stand "outside oneself."

If team sports offer boys the opportunity to learn about collaboration and competition, what does experience teach their sisters about these same things?

Hennig and Jardin think that girls tend to define competence quite differently than boys do. For the traditional woman, competence is demonstrated by marrying a competent man, after winning him away from her competitors, other girls. For the achievement-oriented adolescent girl, the conflict between the desire to develop her own potential and the perceived need to find a mate through whom she can experience competence by proxy is often traumatic. There is tremendous social pressure on young girls to measure success in terms of popularity rather than personal accomplishment. For this reason, Hennig and Jardin set about the task of finding commonalities among twenty-five women who entered the work force in the 1920s and 1930s and ended up holding top executive positions. To further explore the dynamics of successful achievement-oriented behavior in those women, they assessed the youthful experience that enabled these women to succeed in male-dominated professions. Hennig and Jardin hypothesized that they had sidestepped the traditional roadblocks experienced by so many other women. They found significant similarities:

1. Each woman was either the eldest of female children or the only child.
2. Fathers and daughters shared interests traditionally regarded as appropriate only for fathers and sons: physical activity, the acquisition of outdoor skills, an aggressive wish to achieve and a willingness to compete. (One wonders if these treasures would have been offered the girl if there had been a brother around!)
3. During adolescence, the father placed great importance on his daughter's developing skills and abilities. Admiration and affection flowed from father to daughter on the basis of objective accomplishment and success. In addition, there is no evidence that the father in any way rejected the daughter's femininity.
4. The parents, especially the father, were the daughter's major source of support. In fact, when these women felt rejected or isolated for holding different values and standards than their peers, they sought the consolation of their families and therefore never lost a sense of their "all-rightness."

Certainly the information about these twenty-five women is valuable, yet it leads us to the question: what about the thousands of women who did not have these experiences growing up? What were some of the contributing factors that influenced them to choose more traditional roles?

One of the first places to look is girls' attitudes toward success and winning. Matina Horner, in her famous studies of female college students, concluded that women are threatened by success because outstanding academic or other competitive achievement activities are consciously or unconsciously equated with loss of femininity. The women were also fearful of what their success would ultimately cost them.

Girls learn early to avoid winning because they don't want to deal with the perceived negative consequences. A recent situation brought this home. Several of us were talking to a friend whose daughter Amy just won the lead in the school play. She said Amy's friends were now angry at her, leaving Amy very upset about the "success." But do boy football players get angry at the guy who makes team captain? Usually not — because they *need* to depend on him and support him. After all, the better he is, the better they all are. In this instance, instead of getting support, Amy was treated in a hostile manner by her friends until she became apologetic for winning. Then she was allowed back into the circle. These early experiences are very powerful, and the lessons are well-learned by most women. Just think for a minute—how many times have you discounted your strengths? Made self-deprecating statements when given a compliment? ("Oh, I really don't do that so well, my friend does it much better!") How often have you stopped yourself from talking about an accomplishment because you didn't want someone else to feel bad?

Are there residual, subliminal ways in which you continue to play the game of self-sabotage while attempting to succeed in the corporate world? Do you try to keep the egos of your male boss, coworkers and staff intact at your own expense? Is your transition fraught with the internal conflict of wanting to "go for it" yourself while still believing that "being a good girl" is the only way to win and share in the opportunities and rewards that exist in the world of work?

No one has to lose. On the contrary, creative capacity and resources expand when individuals with different viewpoints, backgrounds and experiences merge! Sharing power requires all your energy, and you cannot waste it in continually monitoring what you are doing and saying to please other people. You probably are fully aware that winning a place on a work team does not mean winning approval for your personality, your femininity or even yourself. It means winning the respect of your teammates for your abilities and skills. When talking to successful women in male-dominated fields, we are told repeatedly they won their place on the team and the admiration and cooperation of coworkers through competence. Only after proof of their expertise were they treated holistically as workers and as women.

Women's Special Contributions to the Work Place

The rigid boundaries of the man's world have already begun shifting. We are experiencing the birth (albeit a slow and sometimes painful one) of a new "democracy." Look at the statistics of the number of women in middle management. True, there aren't many in top management positions yet, but there is no way to keep those middle managers out of higher positions for long. To change this particular political structure we must all register, vote, participate and be recognized for contributions made to the bottom line. Then and only then will we have the opportunity to change the rules. The challenge is to be clear enough in our own values and aspirations to maintain them while moving into positions of power.

The following questions need to be asked by every woman seeking a life in corporate America: How do I gain access to positions of power without losing my individual identity and integrity? What are the values I hold about working with others?

What standards do I have for my boss, teammates and organization? How do I foster worker growth and productivity? It is true that businesses exist to make a profit and you work to earn a living, but the question remains: How do you play the game in such a way that human values and resources are developed and encouraged?

To capture our multiple options, it is necessary to explore how women can change the face of working America by reframing many of the so-called negative female behaviors as positive. Certainly we need to learn from our male colleagues the behaviors of sportsmanship that include the positive aspects of conflict, confrontation and competition. However, we also need recognition for our abilities to manage, organize, intuit and cooperate — abilities that we might well possess *because* we were raised female. Not all sex-role characteristics are negative. As we mentioned before, it is the ability to *choose* behaviors in a given situation that empowers. Only when so-called feminine behaviors are involuntary and self-limiting are they damaging. As Alice Sargent so succinctly puts it in her article "Training for Androgyny," "The truly effective group member is someone who possesses both leadership skills and supporting and helping behaviors, who has both masculine independence and feminine nurturing." Anne Wilson Schaef makes a strong statement in her book *Women's Reality: An Emerging Female System in a White Male Society*. She believes our skills in the area of collaborative peer relationships are sorely needed in the man's world. Schaef feels our knowledge of cooperation will teach men how to share power, which, in her hypothesis, they don't know how to do now.

Schaef elaborates on the difference between the White Male System's and the Female System's definition of a peer relationship: "In the White Male System, relationships are conceived of as being either one up or one down." In other words, when two people encounter each other, the White Male System assumption is that one of them must be superior and the other inferior. In the Female System, relationships are philosophically conceived of as peer relationships, each new encounter holding the promise of equality. She refers to a situation common in the business world: a White Male System person meets a Black or a woman, a person who is *supposed* to go one down, but doesn't. When this happens, the Black or woman is labeled "uppity." According to White Male System thinking, when the supposedly inferior person refuses to kowtow, then the White Male himself goes one down, and he bitterly resents this. The White Male System person believes that true peer or collaborative relationships are impossible; in this hierarchical society, the only options are being one up or one down.

Initially, this theory seems harsh, yet the two of us remember a time when one of us was going to write a book with a male boss. The relationship would have been one of joint contribution, yet the male boss refused to be a coauthor. He insisted that his name go first, and that the title read John Doe with Jane Doe, rather than John Doe and Jane Doe. It was impossible for him to conceive of an employee deserving equal credit in a joint project.

Needless to say, the book never got written because it was too frustrating even to get a clear contract. We went on working together, boss and employee, for several more months. In fact, we worked together well as long as we maintained the one up/one down rule of the White Male System relationship. In the end, at least as far as the book was concerned, it became a lose/lose.

Another area to reframe from negative to positive is the seemingly conflicting needs in women for both achievement and affiliation or popularity.

Judith Bardwick, author of the *Psychology of Women,* asks: "Does a person strive to achieve because he has an internal standard of excellence, a self-image and feeling of self-esteem dependent on how he perceives himself performing — or does he achieve primarily to receive praise from others? Repeatedly, the literature says that girls are generally more dependent, conformist, persuadible and vulnerable to interpersonal rejection than boys." But really, can't we have it both ways? Can't we assume that high-achievement needs (competence and excellence leading to competitive behavior) and high-affiliation needs (praise and acceptance leading to collaborative behavior) can exist harmoniously? Of course they can, and they do — and in this lie the seeds of personal power in today's female worker. Precisely because of our affiliation needs, we bring some very special qualities to the marketplace. From strong affiliation needs comes the skill so often labeled "women's intuition" (the ability to observe and react to subtle nuances of nonverbal behavior) — a very useful team behavior. Sensitivity and awareness of others are essential in building strong collaborative relationships. There are times when the underlying, interpersonal dynamics of a relationship are more responsible for a task's ultimate success than the technical skill either party brings.

Women's affiliation needs have often been cast into the negative frame of "dependence." Yet if these become proactive rather than reactive behaviors, then the need to affiliate becomes one of *choosing* reinforcements. We call it a *support system;* many people in the women's movement have called it *networking.* Whatever the label, it can certainly prove useful to have reliable support, whether it takes the form of a once-a-month professional meeting or a daily encounter with a colleague. By validating each other's work we support each other's strengths, laying a foundation for taking risks and exploring new areas, and thus increasing productivity. For generations mothers have worked to establish a climate where children feel safe to put their best foot forward, to accept challenges that will ensure quality performance. Surely these are some of the very same behaviors that foster productivity in work teams.

And how about *physiological* differences between men and women? Or to put it more bluntly: what effect do hormones have on our performance?

Dr. Melvin Konner, a biological anthropologist for Harvard University, writes an interesting chapter on the subject in his book *The Tangled Wing.* He states that aggressive behavior, linked to the male hormone testosterone, is observed earlier and more frequently in males. Nurturing behavior, linked to the female hormones estrogen and progesterone, is observed more frequently in females. The research he cites repeatedly shows some physiological base for gender-different behavior. Why this gender-different behavior is as broad-based as we see it in this culture, or why it seems to determine one group's acquisition of power over another group, is not accounted for. What is stated is that in both animal and human research males and females express themselves differently in terms of aggression and nurturance. So what does this mean?

Konner concludes: "If the community of scientists whose word and knowledge come to agreement on this point (basic physiological differences between male-female on the aggressive-nurturing continuum), then it seems to me that one policy implication is plausible: Serious disarmament may ultimately necessitate an increase in the proportion of women in government." He cautions that reviewing the records of female rulers is in this connection a useless exercise. "Such women have invariably been embedded in, and bound by, an almost totally masculine power structure and have gotten where they were by being unrepresentative of their gender. Some women are, of course, as violent as any man. But speaking of averages — central tendencies, as the statisticians call them — we can have little doubt that we would all be safer if the world's weapons systems were controlled by average women instead of average men." Hats off to Melvin Konner for expressing so powerfully what we so deeply feel.

The Specific Steps To Collaboration

Two organizational consultants, Daryl R. Conner and Charles L Palmgren, provide a very useful model describing three types of working relationships:

1 + 1 < 2 Self-destructive (negative competitive)
One plus one is less than two.

$1 + 1 = 2$ Static
One plus one equals two.
$1 + 1 >$ Synergistic (collaborative)
One plus one is greater than two.

The $1 + 1 < 2$, or self-destructive relationship, is that in which two people interact in such a way that they consume resources at a greater level than they create benefits. The result is less productive than if they had worked independently. An example of this would be a production department and a sales department of the same company working in opposition to one another, both protecting their turf, miscommunicating, and blaming one another. They resemble two competitors rather than two departments in the same company. They actually have a negative production level.

The $1 + 1 = 2$, or static relationship is one in which both parties consume resources at about the same rate they contribute back to the system. The result is a production output level equal to what would be expected when two components combine their efforts. Initially, this type of working relationship looks fine. However, if there are any unforeseen stresses, circumstances or events that upset this delicate balance in the slightest, then the system can shift into a $1 + 1 < 2$ relationship. In other words, static relationships have no reserves from which they can draw to meet unanticipated demands.

$1 + 1 > 2$, or a synergistic working relationship, is one in which the human components of a system interact in such a way that they consume resources at a level less than what they contribute back to the organization. The result is more productive than if the two had worked independently. Examples of synergistic teams abound. Championship sports, a management team that encourages and develops the skills of each of its members, and a marriage wherein both partners freely contribute to a common goal are all synergistic systems.

What are the necessary conditions to facilitate the $1 + 1 > 2$ synergistic relationship? Many experts in the fields of organizational behavior, psychology and negotiation have addressed this question, and there appear to be some common threads that weave through each of the theories. We call them the ABCs of building team behavior.

The ABCs of Building Team Behavior

A. Assess
   - Clearly assess the situation and identify the issues that need attention.
   - Pinpoint the specific goal, or objectives to be achieved.
B. Brainstorm
   - Generate options, ideas and strategies to achieve the identified goals.
   - Look at the issues in as many ways as possible to elicit *many* options.
   - Do not make judgments as to the value of the suggestions. This will be counterproductive to the brainstorming process.
   - Value diversity and difference of opinion.
C. Consider
   - Carefully consider each suggestion on its own merit. Take care not to reject premature suggestions that seem off-base. Explore each thoroughly, and maybe you'll find an innovative approach.
   - Actively listen to each member's contributions to assure full participation.
D. Decide and Implement
   - Choose those options that seem likely to achieve the identified objectives.
   - Merge differing opinions and ideas to achieve a broad working perspective and plan.
   - Use objective criteria as often as possible to settle differences.
   - Identify those issues and concepts that should not be integrated into the plan.

- Establish specific actions to implement the plan.
- Assign individual members to specific tasks.
- Implement the plan at a speed that respects all parties.

E. Evaluate
  - Monitor progress and supply necessary reinforcements.
  - Refer to the objective criteria when evaluating the success of varying strategies.
  - Monitor feelings to facilitate teamwork, but don't use them as objective criteria for the project's success.

If there is a possibility of team conflict, keep the issues specific and within working boundaries. Roger Fisher, a Harvard lawyer, says "In some ways issue control is much more important than arms control. In conflict situations, to keep the issues specific and honed down will give the parties better management potential than if they had large and varied issues and many weapons." Fisher, with William Ury in their book *Getting to Yes,* reframes the process of negotiating into one of collaborating. They suggest, rather than choose opposing sides on an issue, you present your concerns as a way to inform the other party of the process behind your position. This clearer understanding will foster a climate to generate potential solutions between you and your negotiating partner.

The Harvard Negotiation Project, a series of simulated negotiations by Harvard student negotiating teams which Fisher and Ury were involved in, consistently reinforces the need for care, concern and understanding in dealing with people in teams. Statements such as "How you see the world depends on where you sit"; "The cheapest concession you can make to the other side is to let them know they have been heard," "Understanding is not agreeing. You can understand perfectly and disagree completely"; and "Be hard on the problem, soft on the people"; all capture the most significant element in working with people: the human one.

In exploring the potential of men's and women's collaborating behavior in the workplace, many possibilities emerge. First, if we bring unique skills in addition to those we have in common, then there is a greater pool of resources from which to build a $1 + 1 > 2$ synergistic relationship. Second, each can teach and share skills with the other. This will enhance the creative potential of the individual, thereby increasing the contribution to the team and organization. Third, those systems that function synergistically do so by moving beyond the delicate balance of just "managing." Those who promote collaborative systems know that whenever part of any population or person is not allowed to emerge, the entire system loses due to the energy it takes both to oppress and to fight the oppression. Cutting off any part of yourself, whether nurturing, assertive or competitive, will surely weaken you.

8. Personal/Professional Balance

Thinking about personal-professional balance reminds me of my flight home from Washington, D.C., a couple of years ago. My four-month-old son had finally fallen asleep in my lap and I could reflect on the last thirty-six hours. Despite my exhaustion my mind wouldn't stop reworking the last day and a half, because I desperately needed to understand how I had gotten myself to this point of feeling so overwhelmed and defeated, especially when I had anticipated the opposite.

A few months earlier, I had accepted a contract to conduct five seminars in cities on the East Coast. My naivete and enthusiasm about babies and motherhood led me to believe that if I organized things well enough, there should be no problem in bringing my nursing infant with me. Weeks prior to the first seminar, I made numerous phone calls to friends in D.C. to arrange for a reliable sitter to come to my room in the hotel while I ran the seminar in a large conference room downstairs. Crib, clothing, food and transportation had all been carefully planned for. And I was well-prepared for the seminar, which I had conducted many times in the past. I looked forward to the trip, anticipating a sense of pride and satisfaction in my ability to manage and integrate so well these important aspects of my life. I recalled with a smile the magazine picture my mother had shown me which she said reminded her of me — a woman carrying a baby in one arm and a briefcase in the other.

But on the plane home, pride and satisfaction were far from my mind. Instead I was agonizing over the events of the last day and a half. Why hadn't I realized that a baby could break out in an unidentifiable rash without a moment's notice? How was it that my luggage full of diapers, formula, baby clothes and a business suit could be lost enroute to Washington?

Didn't I know that a baby might not sleep in a strange environment and that conducting an all-day seminar on three hours sleep was torture? Not to mention the difficulty of instantaneously switching gears back and forth from nurturing, calming mother to energized, efficient professional. Why hadn't someone told me? The truth is someone probably did, but I didn't want to hear anything that would discourage me from my dreams of "doing it all." Finally I had my long-awaited family and my blossoming career — I wanted to be fully immersed in both, not to miss a beat in either experience.

It took this thirty-six hours to bring me to the realization that I couldn't keep adding things to my life without letting go of other things. Choices and compromises needed to be made. Priorities must be set. The realization brought a certain relief, the kind you get when you know you've gotten to a truth. But it also brought sadness. What could I let go of? What compromises could I accept? What do I put first and when? Such difficult questions, and ones I admit I still struggle to fully answer.

— AL

Growing up, I associated love and recognition with work and praise. I can't remember receiving love for such personal qualities as being playful or having fun, or later, for being sexual and womanly (all personal qualities) but for the professional qualities of being efficient, ambitious, and self-reliant. I remember receiving praise from my brothers and sisters when I paid for my own college education, because I was independent and fought for what I wanted.

Given that I associate love, recognition and credit with hard work, given that these are the rewards of life I most value and, also, given that having a child does not appear to qualify as hard work in the framework I have set up, it is no surprise I had such difficulty fitting having a child into my career.

A friend recently asked me several questions that brought home to me how deeply entrenched the relationship between work and love (and other rewards) is in my mind. Several of these questions continue to run through my mind:

— Would I be willing to love a child while I was not working?

— Would I be willing to allow someone to love me if I were not working?

— Would I be willing to love me while I was not working?

Later, in listing all the circumstances I must have in my life in order for me to love someone else or be loved by someone else, then eliminating from that list all but the most essential, I again determined I would not be willing to love or have love outside the context of hard work. It is clearly, deeply entrenched in my personal programming.

I feel I must work hard to survive, to stay in control and to make money to be loved. The voice of my father rings in my head: "Don't let anyone get the best of you. Don't depend on anyone. Don't trust anyone. Especially don't trust or depend on men."

I have internalized these messages and made them my own, but I question whether I really want them to run my life and determine the world I live in. My father is many years dead, I have married and moved a thousand miles from that home, yet I still carry those messages as though they were precious jewels I must protect at all cost.

And the cost cannot be ignored — it is feeling forced to choose between a career and a home. One or the other? I've finally decided having to choose one and lose the other is much too costly, I want both. So I continue to ask:

— Am I willing to love myself without working for it?

— Am I willing to love my partner without his having to work for it?

— Am I willing to love a child without the child having to work for it?

— Am I willing to create a reality in which I can have career, child, and loving relationship with my husband?

As I approach raising our first child, I am struggling with the idea of being a child again myself and raising myself in a reality where the rewards are not so firmly and solely attached to hard work. Where the rewards are not for, but in living, loving, playing (yes, and working). Where the rewards are not really rewards so much as gifts of love freely given — to myself for myself, for being me.

Then (I tell myself), only then, will I allow myself to love someone else for free.

— DAL

After nearly two decades of struggle to take control of her own image, body, and life; to make her own choices and discover her own identity; and to gain access to male-dominated positions of power; today's woman is experiencing a new kind of disillusionment.

Surprisingly enough, this is not the disillusionment that comes with the awareness that there is still a long way to go in the struggle for equality. Women seem to acknowledge both the progress that has been made and the need for more. The disillusionment lies in the anticipated *rewards*. We expected our victories to empower us with a greater sense of freedom and control; instead we feel depowered, and more confined than ever. It is becoming clear that in freeing ourselves from restrictive sex roles, stereotypes and myths, we have fallen into a new trap: the Superwoman Syndrome. This syndrome has developed from the mistaken idea that we can and should have it all — partner, home, family, career, social involvement, continued education —

without cost and without breaking stride. Human beings unfortunately don't have super powers, and increasing numbers of would-be superwomen are experiencing feelings of bitterness and failure, finding life a near-impossible juggling act that entails costly sacrifices to themselves, their families and their careers, with few clear solutions in sight.

Today's working woman experiences stresses different from those faced by women of earlier generations, and different from those faced by men in corresponding jobs and positions. Although in the past American women have worked outside the home in great numbers, never before have they strived for a share of the power. For many working women, it is no longer all right merely to participate in the work force — we want to be in leadership roles and positions of authority which enable us to formulate policies and make decisions. Today's working women are pioneers; we are breaking new ground every day, with few role models for guidance.

The few women who achieved positions of leadership in the past paid dearly for their success. They had to choose to go it alone, without support from husbands, children, or even close women friends. These were determined women, willing to pay the price of alienation and isolation.

Of the women attending our professional development seminars, only about a fourth say their mothers had full-time, paying jobs outside the home, and half of these working mothers were employed in traditional female jobs such as nurse, teacher and secretary.

It is easy to understand why today's woman feels besieged. She often leads a "double" life, as devoted homemaker and upwardly mobile career woman. At the best of times she may see herself as a juggler, concentrating on keeping her many duties cycling smoothly. At other times she feels out of control, as her two conflicting roles play tug-of-war with her life. Many women in today's work force are expected — by themselves, as well as by the rest of society — to successfully handle these two major roles. No previous generation of women has been confronted with so many opposing demands, possibilities and expectations.

These expectations differ from those society puts on men. Whereas women spend much energy attempting to manage home and career, men have traditionally used personal life as a support for their professional lives. A recent Stanford University study conducted by Harvey Weinstein and Laraine Zappert indicates that women managers are far more likely than men to experience nightmares, depression and stress and are four times as likely to seek psychological help. This indicates that they are under a kind of strain most men do not experience. It is much harder for the working woman to avoid worry about what's hapìening at home than for her male counterpart.

Another reason for stress overload is that society does not yet fully support women in the working world. Women still earn considerably less than men who perform the same jobs (currently, fifty-nine cents to a man's dollar) and tend not to get promotions or opportunities for advancement as often as men. Also, little has been done to provide adequate daycare for children with working parents, a problem left largely for working mothers to solve.

Despite the stresses, more than half of all women work, and women continue to enter the work force at an unprecedented rate, partly for reasons of economic necessity and partly because they want to. Women have long realized that each new role carries many benefits along with its obligations; the more roles you have, the more privileges you have, and as you acquire more roles, you become more valuable to others. Being appreciated and recognized contributes to strong self-confidence. The demands for equality from women and other minorities include a demand for access to the profits and pleasures of role accumulation. The answer, then, is to find active ways to manage choices happily and profitably. During the ten years in which we have been conducting workshops we have seen the ranks of Superwomen grow geometrically. Workshop participants very often are mothers, wives, students and active community members, as well as committed career women. Among their goals in attending the workshop is to find a balance between their personal and professional lives, to learn to manage the stress they feel on and off the job, and to gain a renewed sense of power and satisfaction in their lives. Through the experiences these women have shared with us we have gained a clearer perspective on the Superwoman Syndrome.

The Superwoman Syndrome

The Superwoman Syndrome is characterized by an unrealistic assessment of time, energy and responsibilities. The Superwoman operates in the belief that she can and must do everything herself. She is committed to perfection in each of her chosen roles. She is driven to get tasks completed at all costs, and when she's finished, she tells herself she could have done better. The constant pressure of "do more, be quicker, neater, smarter" often leaves the Superwoman feeling frustrated, angry and unrecognized. The cycle has internal and external dimensions. Internally, if Superwoman is unsatisfied with her work — and she is seldom satisfied — she does not experience the sense of achievement she should derive from her extraordinary efforts. Externally, because she doesn't let others in on the process of what she's doing, she doesn't get the recognition she desires, and too often is left wondering why others haven't noticed how much time and work have gone into her accomplishments. The multiple commitments Superwoman makes and her tendency to move so quickly from one role to the next often leave her without the support she needs to continue functioning at her top level of performance.

She responds to "shoulds" and expectations so completely that she neglects her own physical and emotional needs. Inevitably the costs of this behavioral style are resentment, isolation and burnout. The worst of it is that, after a while, no matter how much she accomplishes, she still doesn't feel like Superwoman. In her fantasy, the internal "movie" of her life, she may triumph, but, in real life, the moment of glory never comes. There is always more to do.

There are three major phases to the Superwoman Syndrome: commitment, action, and burnout. Each phase is built on an incorrect assessment of reality.

Phase 1: Commitment

The saga begins as the fledgling Superwoman chooses her roles and takes on their many duties. At minimum, she becomes involved with her job, partner, home, children and community and the multiple tasks and duties that accompany each. The underlying message to herself in the commitment stage is "I want to have a home, family, and career, and to do my very best at everything I try." At this point, like a kid in a candy store, she is excited by all of the opportunities and potential rewards she sees and chooses several directions to pursue actively.

Along with the excitement, Superwoman feels a genuine sense of gratitude for the chance to assume a variety of roles. She often has a fantasy of the rich and fulfilling life that will be hers as she reaps the rewards of recognition, status and power from her career, as well as affection, appreciation and intimacy from her family. "I could picture happy home scenes," described one woman, "where the whole family was gathered in loving closeness around a table of superbly prepared food in an immaculately clean kitchen — all my doing, of course — and everyone was eager to hear my latest triumphs at work. The most striking thing about the fantasy when I think about it now is that everything is always in order and everyone is always smiling."

Another woman, an accountant with a large company and the mother of two small sons, told us "I knew it wouldn't be easy, but I kept telling myself how proud I would be for being able to do it all. So whenever the opportunity came along for me to take on new responsibilities, I did so willingly — always grateful for the opportunity to prove myself, whether it was a new project at work, a school activity for the boys, or entertaining friends at our home. I wanted to see myself as invincible — the perfect wife, mother and professional."

Further encouragement at this phase is provided by the role models Superwoman finds among her own ranks. She seeks proof through the performance of other women that multiple commitments are possible. One woman admitted to a sense of elation when she could point to another who was managing all of her many roles well, or appeared to be. "My motto was, you can always make time for the things you really want to do. This allowed me a handy explanation as to why other women *couldn't* do it all — they just didn't really *want* to."

At this stage, Superwoman sees only the reinforcement for her choices. She sifts out any information that suggests she might be taking on too much by herself and focuses instead on evidence in her environment that supports her belief that she can meet all the expectations of a career-minded professional and still maintain primary responsibility for the domestic needs of the household.

Phase 2: Action

Having made her choices and committed herself, Superwoman tackles the challenges of her many roles with a high level of energy, commitment and enthusiasm. She not only meets these challenges admirably, but also is sensitive and responsive to the standards and expectations of those around her. Although she sometimes feels pressured and overburdened, she strongly believes she must do everything herself, and expects a minimal amount of support and assistance from the people around her. Soon Superwoman is working feverishly all the time.

When Stephanie, a homemaker, returned to the work place full time after her children entered school, she found herself going nonstop from 4:30 A.M. to 10:00 P.M. Analyzing her behavior, she said she didn't want to deprive her family of homemade bread, a garden, and a clean house just because she

Using Personal Power to
Counteract the Superwoman Syndrome

Needed Awareness	Needed Skills
Phase 1: Commitment Knowing what's really important to you, what you really want Being aware of how much actual time it will take you to carry out the activity you choose Knowing how skilled you are at the activity: Assessing whether you have the energy to take on this activity and do it to your standards Assessing how important this activity is to your goals and priorities	Assign priorities to your goals, both personal and professional The ability to say no to those demands on your time and energy which conflict with your priorities and goals
Phase 2: Action Foreseeing the busier times in your schedule Being aware of the effects of your schedule on you and those around you Knowing who in your environment is a potential source of support Identifying tasks that can be eliminated, turned over to others, or abbreviated Assessing whether the time and energy you spend is worth the payoffs you receive or the inconvenience incurred	Planning ahead and projecting busy times Asking for help Delegating tasks and activities to others Developing and maintaining a support system Replenishing yourself through relaxation and recreation
Phase 3: Burnout Awareness of your individual signals of overstress (e.g. headaches, fatigue, confusion, irritation, insomnia) Pinpointing the sources of stress in your life Awareness of your individual emotional, physical and spiritual needs Identifying available resources to help you manage stress (books, counselors, classes, friends, family)	Managing stress overload Reevaluating priorities Reestablishing loyalty to priorities Setting new directions

decided to work full time. In taking on new activities it hadn't yet occurred to her to give up some of the old ones or get some help from family members. Superwoman at this stage is motivated by two main factors: a feeling of pride in her independence and resourcefulness, and a sense of her indispensability; everyone needs her, and she is in demand everywhere she looks. Power and control, two long-awaited rewards of modern woman, are finally hers!

Most women tell us that, in retrospect, they see that their feelings of disenchantment really began at this point. In a life devoted to job, home, children, and friends, Superwoman realizes there aren't enough hours in the day to do everything she's planned. Desperately attempting to solve her problem, she convinces herself that she just needs to be better organized. She hates to think she can't fulfill all her obligations. "My life was dominated by list-making, rushing around, and sleepless nights of planning," reported one woman. "I was in a crisis state, really panicked. But I didn't admit to anyone — not even myself — that I felt this frightened. Somehow I felt that having a hard time was a statement of my inadequacy. I couldn't see giving up anything, or asking for help either. Instead of saying no to extra demands, I just speeded up."

Now the problem is exacerbated by the fact that Superwoman is beginning to betray her own standards of excellence. Even if by some miracle she is getting all her tasks done, she can no longer adhere to her perfectionist expectations. In many cases, Superwoman has no time to see how she is handling her multitudinous duties. Seldom in her busy schedule does she allow herself to experience the out-of-control feeling of being caught on a fast moving train that she doesn't know how to slow down. "I felt as if I had tunnel vision. All my energy was devoted to preparing myself for the next task. I really noticed how out of touch I was when a friend commented one day on the horrible rainy weather we'd been having and I didn't know what she was talking about. I had been so out of touch with my surroundings I hadn't even noticed."

Superwoman's pride in herself eventually gives way to a pervasive sense of guilt and defeat, taking her to phase three, burnout.

Phase 3: Burnout

Superwoman is now in a painful dilemma, caught between her overzealous sense of responsibility and her obsessive desire to do everything perfectly. She sees no way out but to continue to honor the commitments she has made, while paying less and less attention to her dwindling supply of energy. Her control over her daily life is long gone. She is now driven by what seem to be superhuman demands. To make things worse, this crisis has also triggered her worst possible fears — failure of her ability to do competently all those things she said she would do. How do all those people who depend on her feel about her now? How does she feel about herself?

One woman told us "I suspected that the people around me — my family, friends, coworkers — were disappointed with me because I was not coming through in ways I had promised. Any upset the kids experienced, I attributed to my inability to really be there with them. Any mistake I made at work did a job on my feelings of confidence. I started to feel like a fraud, and was very frightened I would be found out. The unspoken feeling of doom was always with me — at any moment my inadequacy as wife, mother, and worker would be discovered. And I hated the feeling. I began to feel very angry: I had worked so hard for this?"

The feelings of isolation and resentment reach a crescendo at this stage. Superwoman, unable to let others see her fear and self-doubt, shows only her tension and anger. She perceives others as a source of demand and criticism rather than as a source of support. And, in fact, support does not come easily from those around her because she has taught them she can do it all herself. Her tense and angry exterior encourages others to keep their distance. Everyone, including Superwoman, feels that no amount of appreciation, gratitude or assistance is enough to break the vicious cycle her attitudes and actions perpetuate.

Superwoman and Society

At one time Superwoman was an extreme type. However, as more and more women juggle multiple roles, *not* being Superwoman is the exception. The central issue in the Superwoman Syndrome is the interplay between what the woman expects of herself and what society expects of her. Superwoman is an extension of the old stereotype of woman as homemaker. According to this view, a woman should take primary responsibility for childcare, home maintenance and traditional wifely duties. The revised version of the stereotype allows a woman to work outside the home so long as she still fulfills the responsibilities society has assigned her as helpmate and homemaker. The stereotype is doubly inflexible, in that it requires simultaneously that the traditional woman's role remain intact and that career roles make no allowances for mothering and homemaking. As a result, women feel cornered into either-or choices or pressured into managing both home and work as if the other didn't exist.

Though many women think they should not have to accept the traditional woman's role, they can't help feeling guilty if they don't. In addition, they quite naturally want the rewards and intimacies associated with home and family. Consequently, in an unconscious attempt to justify taking on their new work role, they strive extraordinarily hard for excellence in the traditional woman's role. If their homemaking is unimpeachable, they reason, then no one will be able to criticize or question them for involvement in other enterprises. This leaves them trying to live two lives, and the clearcut separation between professional and personal life makes it virtually impossible to negotiate or trade off between the two when conflicts arise. People at work and at home have been encouraged to expect Superwoman to keep these two lives separate, and are therefore unlikely to be seriously concerned or helpful when the tug-of-war becomes too much for her.

The message to women today seems to be that if you choose to work (with the implication that the choice is based on whim rather than on legitimate financial, intellectual or emotional factors), then you must suffer the stress that accompanies filling multiple roles. This attitude is manifested on a variety of levels. In the home it is seen in the lack of responsibility taken by other family members to see that domestic duties are fairly shared. In the workplace, it is reflected in the reluctance of companies and organizations to consider flexible schedules for both male and female workers, childcare subsidies, and on-site childcare facilities. (A recent survey by Catalyst, a non-profit organization that aids working women, revealed that, of 374 major companies polled, only 1 percent had on-site daycare, only 7 percent offered subsidies for childcare, and only 37 percent had instituted flexible work hours.) On the government level, little progress has been made toward offering encouragement through tax incentives for companies and communities to develop good childcare programs.

Restructuring

If we are to do away with the Superwoman Syndrome, we must challenge the expectations held by our mates, children, employers and legislators, as well as those we ourselves hold that perpetuate the no-win demands placed on women.

Recognizing and Respecting Limits

Every Superwoman must recognize that there is no such thing as "having it all." With every gain in your life there will be some loss. Being willing to make choices and to let go of some activities in order to take on others is the only realistic way to find personal-professional balance. On the other hand, you can have it all—if what that means is partner, children and career—if you are willing to pace your efforts and sacrifice some traditional expectations.

We all have limits. A characteristic of the personally power-ful person is the ability to recognize, accept, and respect those limits. No matter how quickly or efficiently we move, there will never be enough time to do all the worthwhile and important things in life. Putting yourself on the track to personal-profes-sional balance requires that you be able to say no to the excessive requests and expectations of others and to your own unrealistic expectations.

Saying no may be difficult, especially if you have been in the habit of always saying yes. There will be guilt feelings to deal with and anxiety about losing the goodwill of others. There may be disappointment when you admit to yourself you can't be per-fect, all-giving, and all-doing. And for many women there will be the fear that *if you are not indispensable you will be dispensed with.* But only if you adhere to the realistic parameters of your own capabilities can you claim to be in charge of your own life.

As a nurse in Colorado put it, "I spent so many years of my life saying yes to other people's wants that I lost the ability to know what *I* wanted any more. I used to believe that no one could manage well without me. So it was yes, I'll serve on this commit-tee, and yes, I'll drive you and your friends to the skating rink, and yes, I'll work a double shift, on and on, ad nauseam. It was a neat little ego trip I was on — while I was feeling resentful, I could also feel super-important. Now that I say no more often, I don't hear people saying 'We can always count on you, Marie' or 'How do you do it all? You're amazing.' But what I do get is a chance to ask myself what *I* want and to know that when I do say yes it's because I choose to. That's been a real revelation for me — that only when I learned to say no, did I also learn to say yes sincerely."

Reestablishing Loyalty to Priorities and Values

Some women caught in the Superwoman trap have either forgotten their priorities or never clarified them in the first place. The energy drain caused by nondirected behavior is a major source of frustration and stress. The feeling is similar to running on a treadmill — a lot of activity but no progress. If you don't know what's really important to you, it is extremely easy to end up spending your time on those tasks and activities that are easiest and quickest — and yet have little or no pay-off for you personally or professionally.

In establishing loyalty to priorities, it is important to distinguish long-range goals from short-term ones. Too often Superwoman will mortgage her time away on day-to-day responsibilities that are less important to her than her long-range goals. She desperately wants to believe that all the things she values can be priorities. May, a journalist who was committed to the long-term advancement of her career, found herself at the burnout phase largely because of her tenacious belief that she could continue to earn a significant income as a teacher and make major advances in her career as a journalist at the same time. In restructuring, she realized the only way to release herself from the Superwoman Syndrome was to make some choices. She decided to cut down on her teaching so she could devote more time to writing. She gave up a portion of her income in order to reap the future benefits of long-range career advancement.

Choosing priorities can feel like a gamble. You hope you are choosing well for yourself and those affected by your choices, and that you won't regret the things to which you assigned secondary importance. When the tally is in, even well-thought-out choices will reveal their fair share of both costs and benefits. There is no way to avoid the costs. The Superwoman who hopes she can avoid paying the costs of choices by not setting priorities in the first place inevitably discovers she had made choices all along. She simply decided not to be conscious of them. Your priorities are revealed not through your words but through your actions. The things you devote your time, energy and best efforts to are those things you are choosing to make priorities, whether or not you acknowledge them.

As an exercise to help you clarify your priorities, make a list of what is most important to you. Ask yourself if you are satisfied with the amount of time and energy and the quality of effort you are devoting to each. What would you like to give more attention to? What are you willing to give less attention to?

Renegotiating Both Spoken and Unspoken Agreements

There will always be times when priorities are not clearcut. An important business appointment conflicts with the needs of a sick child. An offer of a promotion and transfer runs up against a desire to be close enough to help out aging parents. An opportunity to return to school to complete a degree conflicts with the need to bring home a paycheck. The time you must spend on a special work project cuts into the time you have arranged to spend with your family or friends.

Many women report that after they decide on their own priorities they are faced with the difficult task of getting the support of husbands, children, parents, bosses and teachers — all of whom may expect her total commitment.

When Eleanor, the single parent of two teenage boys, decided to return to work after several years as a homemaker, she thought she was doing so with the support of her sons. For years they had been encouraging her to realize her hopes of finding a job and becoming financially independent. However, when the requirements of her job interfered with Eleanor's ability to keep house, prepare their meals, and do their laundry, they complained. The boys did not expect that their mother's commitment to her job would involve a lessening of her commitment to their daily needs, and Eleanor felt betrayed by their reaction.

If women like Eleanor are to avoid the Superwoman trap and gain the support of those with whom they live and work, they must be willing to renegotiate both the spoken and unspoken agreements that affect their lives. Families must bring out into the open their honest expectations of one another and then must formulate new ones based on what each is willing and able to do. For the Superwoman dedicated to pleasing everyone, her challenge will be to withstand the anxiety of disappointing people. She may have to confront the resistance her family has to seeing that her work is as important as her husband's. She may have to convince her employer that her desire to attend to family responsibilities does not mean she is "not serious" about her work.

The major underlying goal is to redefine what we now think of as women's problems as people's problems. Tending to a sick child, maintaining a home, responding to the needs of aging parents are the concerns of all people, not just women. Fulfilling obligations at work and meeting job or career goals are the concerns of all people, not just men.

As more women are able to renegotiate the spoken and unspoken agreements governing their lives, more men will begin to do so also. In *The Second Stage,* Betty Friedan reminds us that "Men as well as women must set up their lives to achieve balance between success in work and gratification in personal life." The trend already reveals that as women move toward fulfillment in the world of work outside the home, more men are recognizing and gravitating toward fulfillment of their desires to share homemaking and child-rearing. However, reversing roles, as many couples have discovered, is not the answer, for the same frustrating limitations prevail no matter who plays the role. The liberation of the sexes will depend on the combined efforts of men and women to disentangle themselves from the limiting definitions of prescribed sex roles. Renegotiating agreements calls for a creative view of new possibilities based on the individual needs, wants and abilities of the people concerned. It will take courage, honesty and trial-and-error to discover what is personally fulfilling, and it will take courage, caring and patience to allow others their own discovery.

We can seek allies not only in our partners, but in our employers, communities and government. Women can direct their support and loyalty toward those employers who institute policies to allow for flexible hours, part-time work, childcare facilities, and individually designed benefit packages to suit family needs; toward communities who support quality neighborhood daycare centers with parent boards overseeing standards; and toward legislators and political candidates who actively campaign to advance the issues facing women and minorities today.

Ability and Willingness To Elicit the Cooperation of Others

Though the number of married women in the work force has greatly increased in the last decade, the number of husbands equally sharing housework has not. Women report that they are seeing more willingness in their spouses to "help them out," but the main responsibility for knowing *when* a task should be done, seeing that it is begun and completed, and that it is done to the agreed-upon standards still rests mainly upon their own shoulders.

The cooperation of those people you live and work with can make all the difference in your ability to balance home, family and career. Superwoman's resistance to making requests and delegating tasks is notorious and is reflected here in the statements of Margaret, a lawyer, mother, wife and homemaker. "My only attempt at delegating responsibilities to my family proved to be a disaster. I thought I'd let my kids — now that they were getting older — take some of the household chores off my shoulders. They were surprisingly willing and told me they wanted to try their hand at cooking dinner, and so I agreed. Well, the first night we had french fries, hot dogs, cola and brownies with ice cream. The next time they cooked we had french fries, hamburgers, cola, brownies and ice cream. After the third meal in a week like this, I fired them. Who can stand by and let her family die of obesity, poor nutrition, or a case of terminal cavities?"

Like Margaret, many Superwomen have difficulty overcoming the initial problems of delegating. When you turn over tasks and responsibilities to others, in most cases you will discover that they will do the task *their* way and not yours. The real art of delegating is having the patience to let others grow competent in the tasks you assign. If you expect too much too soon, you will get frustrated and probably reclaim the responsibility for the task, reconfirming your real belief that "If you want something done right, you have to do it yourself!" This attitude, more than any other, sabotages ability to elicit the cooperation of others.

Getting others to cooperate depends on your willingness to motivate, work with, and reward people for their effort. People are more willing to take on a new responsibility if they agree with the need for it, feel able to do it, are respected for their efforts, and are attracted to the payoffs. Eliciting the cooperation of others will be easier if you can be open about your feelings—not just your frustrations, but also your needs, fears and vulnerabilities. Trying to motivate others by guilt is rarely as effective as motivating them through understanding. People also tend to be committed to goals they have had a share in setting, so inviting others to participate in decision-making is likely to work better than telling them what they have to do. The feedback people receive along the way will greatly influence their continued commitment to a task: Let others know when you are pleased with any part of their effort and be sure they know you are a resource to help them grow more competent.

Remember, change is difficult; we all resist it at times. Your patience and persistence will help. You may need to describe your feelings, reiterate your expectations, offer your input, give feedback several times, before you can truly feel that you have been relieved of a responsibility. In the long run the gains will be worth the effort, both for you and the person you have enabled to grow more competent and responsible.

Commitment to Replenish Your Energy

Perhaps the most challenging part of restructuring your life will be committing yourself to replenish your energy. Most Superwomen put their personal needs aside, so that by the time they reach the burnout phase they have developed a habit of neglecting their physical, emotional, mental and spiritual needs. If that has been your pattern, you may no longer even know what your needs are. Any decision to begin meeting your needs may carry with it confusion, anxiety and guilt. Yet the key to renouncing the self-destructive "do more, faster, better" lifestyle is reclaiming the parts of yourself that were abandoned along the way.

You can enhance the quality of your life and replenish your energy by being wise in what you eat and how you exercise. Certain foods contribute to an inability to cope with stress. For example, a high intake of caffeine, which is found not only in coffee and tea, but also in chocolate, cola, and other soft drinks, has been linked with a stress-prone diet. A good stress-fighting diet minimizes the intake of these foods as well as white flour, sugar, salt, saturated fats, artificial additives, tobacco and alcohol. If you have come to rely on convenience foods, you are probably feeding yourself a diet deficient in necessary vitamins and minerals, which won't support an active life.

Be aware not only of what you eat, but also how you eat it. Many Superwomen approach a meal as if it were one more task to be completed. They grab a cup of coffee in the morning and call it breakfast. Often mealtime is rushed, or used as an opportunity to work. Lunch becomes a business meeting and dinner becomes the time to work out family conflicts. If your nutritional habits are to protect you adequately, you need to maintain your recommended weight, avoid skipping meals, and set aside worries and troubles so that you can have peaceful and leisurely mealtimes.

Like good nutrition, a regular exercise program can protect you against stress. Occasional recreational exercise is fun and helps to release tension, but a regular program of vigorous exercise has a much greater potential for helping replenish your energy. Running, bicycling, fast walking, and swimming are examples of aerobic exercise that increase fitness and endurance.

Learning to relax and training yourself to let go can significantly help you replenish yourself emotionally and mentally. You can learn letting-go techniques that are useful in stressful situations, as well as relaxation techniques that can be practiced regularly.

Handling stressful situations such as high-pressure meetings, job evaluations and public-speaking engagements can be made easier by simply learning to breathe deeply. You may find that closing your eyes and taking ten deep breaths before facing a challenging task will help you to focus and concentrate. Taking a brief walk or performing a few stretching exercises can accomplish a similar calming and letting-go effect. For many people, letting go means being able to find closure on certain events of the day. Finishing old business allows you to move unencumbered to the next task. One way to achieve closure is to complete one task before taking on another, especially during heavy workload periods. Another way is to keep a journal. An emphasis on closure will help you settle conflicts and disagreements as soon as possible rather than carrying them around unresolved.

Committing yourself to practice relaxation techniques is helpful not only in developing long-term protection against the effects of stress but also in contributing to your spiritual development. Meditation as a relaxation technique has been the subject of much research, and has gained considerable popularity and credibility in this country. It takes time to learn to meditate, but anyone can do it. Practicing meditation daily can result in greater clarity of mind, as well as increased ability to cope with the demands of a multicommitted life.

You will find your own special way to relax if you give yourself permission to do so. Almost anything that frees your mind of worries and concerns will work. Most people relax when they do things they enjoy, simply for the pleasure it brings them. You don't always have to work toward self-improvement, and everything needn't be a learning experience. Ironically, like the lost object that finally appears when we have quit looking for it, self-improvement and growth are frequently the unexpected gifts of moments spent enjoying the pleasures of life.

Finally, the value of a strong support system cannot be over-estimated as a means to help you replenish your personal energy. A support system, as described by educator and author Charles Seashore, is a resource pool of people you can call on selectively to support you in a direction of your choice; it leaves you stronger. "Leaves you stronger" — that is the bottom-line criterion for support. Support is individually defined; what feels like support to you may not feel that way to someone else, and the kind of support you want may change according to the situation. Sometimes a good listener makes you feel stronger. At other times you may need someone to help you brainstorm new ideas.

There are many different roles people can play to provide support, and so a well-developed support system encompasses a variety of types of people. In your support system you might want to have people who can act as role models, mentors and sponsors as well as people who share your interests, can empathize with you, are good at challenging you, good at helping you feel respected and are willing and able to problem-solve with you. Some people you know are probably good at providing a variety of support, others are good at offering a single kind.

To keep your support system working, it is important to be clear about what kind of support you want and who can give it to you. It's time to stop seeking support from people who haven't given it to you in the past and are unlikely to give it to you in the future; besides being a waste of time, it is frustrating and may leave you feeling resentful and less positive about yourself. Use your energy to initiate contact and request support from people who are willing and able to share their capabilities and personal resources with you.

9. Empowering One Another

When I think of the concept of empowerment, I remember an opportunity my parents gave me when I was sixteen. My mother wanted to have our den remodeled, but, working full time, she was unable to do it herself. Knowing I had no plans for the summer vacation, she asked me if I would like to take over the project. I was only mildly interested until I began to realize she meant really *take over the whole project, from beginning to end. She told me she would give me a certain amount of money to work with and essentially the rest was up to me. I was to decide what to do with the walls and floor, design cabinets and book-cases, buy furniture, rugs, and drapes, and hire a carpenter to do any work I wanted done. She only asked that I make the room consistent with the rest of the house (I took that to mean no floor to ceiling murals of rock stars) and that I show her my choices in furniture before I purchased any.*

I was thrilled with being given so much responsibility and control over what I saw as an important project. After all, the whole family would be affected by my decisions for a long time. The first thing I did was to call a carpenter who had done some work for my parents before and ask if he would like to work for me. It was a good choice — "Coke" was a short, stocky man who was highly skilled and full of good humor. No doubt he was somewhat amused by the situation, but he was always completely respectful of my role in the project. I have memories of him poking his head in the door at 8:00 sharp every morning shouting, "Hey, Boss, I'm here and ready to go." He never went to my parents with questions or problems, always to me. And he refused to make my decisions for me, even when I asked him to.

Together we ripped up linoleum, sanded the floor, painted ceilings and windows, designed bookcases, cabinets, selected wood and finishes. Together we created a room we were proud of and my parents were very pleased with.

I have always been grateful to my parents and Coke for that experience. I judge it to be one of those fortunate empowering opportunities that has all the more impact because of being well timed. At sixteen, finding out that you can take charge, be trustworthy, decisive and successful is a wonderful feeling with lasting effects on self-image.

— AL

My first job. Fresh out of college, I was eager to be one of the best caseworkers the Center for Young Parents (a school for adolescent pregnant girls) ever hired. I quickly realized that in one's first job, more time is spent learning than actually contributing, and I was fortunate to have an excellent teacher. My experiences with Inez Hedemann, the Director of Social Services at the school, stand out for me — a couple in particular.

Inez never once in the several years we worked together told me I was wrong or gave me advice, even in those cases when I made a glaring fool of myself by flaring up at a staff meeting or making an inappropriate decision in handling a case. Rather, she did something much more effective. After each instance, she would gently ask: "Dolores, what other way could you have handled that situation?" We would spend countless hours discussing the costs and benefits of my actions and the options that I hadn't seen at the time. I didn't realize it then, but Inez was teaching me how to think. She was allowing me to see the effect I could have on my own life if I thought through my actions rather than spending my energy reacting to someone else. I'm still learning this. After I do something and am distraught at the outcome I hear her voice (but now it's mine) ask: "Dolores, what other alternatives were available to you to handle that situation?"

The other event that altered my direction happened one day while observing Inez work. She was counseling a student with multiple family and personal problems. I was awed at the level at which she worked and the positive response of the young woman. After the session, I remarked on how intuitive she was and that I thought she had a gift few people had. She replied that what I observed was her skill; it had developed over years of practice and experience. It was not intuition, and it was nothing mysterious. In fact, she said, if I worked and observed and practiced I could do exactly what she did, and she would help me do it. I always left our conversations feeling empowered and good about myself, confident I could make a difference. When I moved on (at her encouragement) I missed her terribly until I realized that I carried her voice in my head and her spirit in my heart.

— DAL

The preceding chapters have concentrated on the development of concepts and skills that can help women project personal power. The focus has been on what women can do to control and direct our own inner resources in order to succeed in the work place, and also to influence change and receptivity in the people with whom we live and work. Personal power is essential to the success of today's working women.

Nevertheless, every aspiring woman realizes that lack of personal power is not the only roadblock to upward career mobility. The work environment and the organizational structure may also present critical obstacles to a woman's career success. In

Men and Women of the Corporation, Kanter explains that the unbalanced numbers of men and women in groups and the way power and opportunity are distributed have a great deal to do with women's lack of managerial success. In large organizational hierarchies women's opportunities tend to get blocked, we have little power, and, if we do get close to the top, we find few, if any, other women there.

Women's difficulty in achieving upward career mobility is due to an interaction of personal and situational factors. For example, women are often criticized for overemphasizing the task at hand instead of seeing it as one of a series of steps to advancement. One explanation of this behavior is that women lack skill in personal planning and goal-setting. But it is equally reasonable to conclude that since women are not promoted within organizations, we tend to concentrate on the jobs that are assigned to us. When people feel constraints on their opportunity and power, they tend to take fewer risks, have lower aspirations, feel increased stress, have reduced commitment to the organization and greater hostility toward leaders — becoming ineffective in leadership roles themselves. In order for women to succeed in the work place, people-centered strategies, such as the ones described in the preceding chapters, must be combined with situation-centered strategies at the highest organizational level.

Increasing women's opportunities in the work place serves not only the interests of human rights, which by themselves would more than justify action, but also the needs of organizations. Organizations will benefit from making full use of the potential of their 47 million female employees.

If women's access to power and opportunities is to be increased, those in leadership positions will have to use their influence to change the present system. People who have already attained position power have the means to introduce policies, programs and practices to facilitate women's advancement.

Power, however, is something people do not share readily. It is hoarded and guarded as jealously as if there were not enough to go around. This traditional concept of power as a limited resource, upon which the American corporate structure is based, discourages people with position power from helping to make structural changes to empower others.

According to the concept of power as a fixed sum, a gain in power by one person or group must result in a corresponding loss of power for another person or group. Power is equated with the ability to dominate others. Those in positions of power therefore have a stake in keeping it for themselves, because to share it means to lose it.

Forward-thinking individuals in all professions are beginning to define and understand power in a way that lends itself more readily to sharing. Kanter equates power with autonomy and mastery and defines it as "the ability to get things done, to mobilize resources, to get and use whatever it is a person needs for the goals she is attempting to meet." According to this view, the total amount of power in an organization can be increased by generating more autonomy and increasing more peoples' access to resources. In other words, power expands when you share it; one person's gain is not another person's loss.

This is precisely what is meant by empowering. To empower women is to enable us to develop the skills and capabilities that will increase our control over decisions, resources and structures affecting our success. Empowerment is not *power over* others, but *power with* others, following an "I win/you win" strategy. It is using one's ability to release the power in oneself and in others.

People who empower others provide:

- Information, so a person can learn what to do and how to do it.
- Resources, so a person has access to the staff, money and equipment necessary to reach a goal.
- Training opportunities, so a person can develop skills.
- Alternatives, to remove barriers so a person can maneuver through the system.

- Opportunities for decision-making and delegation of responsibilities, so a person can grow more independent.
- Opportunities to make contacts and build alliances, so a person will have the acknowledgement, support and cooperation of others.

Women leaders are in a unique position to help other women. Through their own experience they can understand and identify with the desire to achieve positions of power; they have firsthand experience in overcoming obstacles; and, most important, they are in a position to change the formal and informal systems affecting advancement within an organization. But are women leaders successfully empowering other women?

Almost every aspiring woman has an opinion on this subject, usually based on her own experience with a woman for whom she has worked. Some express gratitude that their rise to success was greatly aided by the support and help of a more experienced woman. Others attribute their lack of success to the limiting, controlling and sometimes hostile behavior of a woman boss. No doubt both situations exist.

Bayes and Newton, writing on women in authority, reflect one viewpoint on women's motivation to help other women. They claim that, because her power is continually challenged, a woman leader may resort to domineering behavior. Moreover, because women have been trained to compete with other women for favored positions with men, it may be difficult for them to join in supporting and protecting other women. A certain number of female executives do suffer from the "Queen Bee syndrome," a set of attitudes that preclude empowering other women. Queen Bees are socially and professionally successful, but are resistant to increasing the number of women in their ranks because they want to preserve their unique status in a man's world. (See Chapter 3.)

On the other hand, there are those who believe that the Queen Bee is quickly becoming an anachronism. Margaret Hennig, coauthor of *The Managerial Woman,* believes that women in senior management are bringing to the surface the pain of their own struggle for success, thus becoming sensitive to the pain of the women under them. "I have kept conscious of the difficulties," they are saying, "I will use my power to unravel the difficulties for my successors" (as quoted in *Ms. Magazine,* December 1982).

The female power style has been described as self-and-people-oriented, expressing a desire to share internal resources and to build interdependent relationships. A study by McClelland and Burnham indicates that successful managers express power in a democratic, coaching style rather than in an authoritarian or coercive way. Women have traditionally used this leadership style in playing the role of family negotiator. As wives and mothers, women have been socialized to serve as sources of strength and support from which others can draw — and this skill can be as valuable in the workplace as in the home.

Empowering Others Increases Personal Power

Perhaps the motivation some women feel to help others comes in part from a basic belief that to empower others is ultimately to empower oneself. It is a belief that as long as women as a whole remain a powerless group, no woman, despite her achievements, titles and success, can be truly powerful. As doors open for one woman, it is likely that more doors will be opened for other women. With every woman who gains control over the decisions, resources and structures affecting her life, all women move a step closer to shared power.

Those who empower others also seem to know that empowering builds bonds. People may give obedience to limiting and controlling bosses, but their loyalties are won by those individuals who enable them to express their potential and to feel proud of their accomplishments. Think of the people in your life to whom you feel most loyal — are they not the ones who offered you the opportunity and means to become who you most want to be? A person who enables others to succeed is invariably sought after and respected. To empower others is to increase your own personal power!

Strategies to Empower One Another

Strategies to help women succeed in career endeavors should obviously respond to the issues that tend to hold women back. The following are general areas in which women can provide empowering opportunities to one another. Some of the specific suggestions offered will only be within the power of those in leadership positions. Other suggestions are within the capability of anyone who is supportive of women's success in the work place.

Empowering through Alliances

Few people make it on their own. If you examine the circumstances behind a person's success, most often you will find he or she has had the backing of key people. Men have long realized that there is truth in the statement "It's not so much *what* you know, but *who* you know that counts," and so have developed a tradition of building contacts, reciprocating favors, and cultivating political savvy in dealing with colleagues. Utilizing alliances seems to be second nature to a great number of business and professional men, whereas women, newer at career strategies, learn the importance of alliances through experience — often the frustrating and disappointing experience of discovering their high performance wasn't enough to earn them advancement.

Networks are gaining recognition among working women as an important means by which to build contacts. Networks are informal groups which serve the purpose of providing information and contacts not easily obtained within formal systems. The existing networks in organizations have long been exclusively male, and women's entry has been difficult and unwelcome. Consequently, women in cities all over the country are forming their own networks — informal groups that meet periodically to pass on professional information, solve problems encountered at work, give references to one another, exchange contacts and favors, and offer information about opportunities and job openings. You can help empower other women and yourself by participating in a women's network. If no such network exists in your city you might consider creating one. A woman who is a leader within an organization is in a unique position to empower other women through creating and participating in a network of aspiring women employees.

A woman can also empower other women by serving as a sponsor or mentor. Advancement within an organization is often dependent on whether a person has had suitable sponsors and mentors throughout his or her career. Unfortunately, many men are reluctant to take on such a role with an aspiring woman, in part because it is viewed as risky and in part because people tend to groom for leadership those people with whom they identify and share common backgrounds. It's no mystery. Most people in leadership roles are men, and they tend to promote other men. This makes it all the more critical that women who have achieved position power choose other women to sponsor or mentor.

In *Paths To Power,* Josefowitz explains that sponsoring and mentoring are two different functions and should be distinguished from each other. Let's take a look. When you sponsor another woman, you use your position power within a system to help her gain visibility and opportunity. You may do this by introducing her to other people in powerful positions. You may speak on her behalf to people who can offer her opportunities to use and gain recognition for her abilities. You may offer her the opportunity to take part in projects and have her join you in special assignments so that her abilities can be seen by others. Simply by letting others know that you back her, you are lending weight to her credibility. You increase her power because your sponsorship indirectly states that you think highly of her abilities and she has access to your resources.

While sponsoring is most often done with a person who has already acquired a level of competency and expertise, mentoring is most helpful to an aspiring woman who has yet to learn the ropes. When you serve as mentor you take on the role of teacher. Your goal is to help increase the competency of your protegee by teaching her how to improve her performance and what she needs to do to have her value recognized by her organization. As a mentor you would sometimes teach specific skills, such as how to make an effective presentation. Other times you would teach strategies, such as which kinds of presentations would be most beneficial to make when and to whom. As a mentor you can help your protegee learn what to do. You may not have the organizational clout a sponsor has, but organizational influence is not a requirement of an effective mentor. In fact, in some circumstances a mentor and protegee may not even be members of the same organization.

You need not have the position power of a sponsor or the expertise of a mentor to be an ally to another woman. Anyone who can point out the pitfalls and short-cuts along the way is in a position to empower. Secretaries and administrative assistants are privy to information that can make all the difference in the world to an aspiring woman's ability to reach her goal. And very often it is the support of peers that contributes most to promoting and shaping careers. By sharing information and strategies, and advising and listening to one another, they help each other as well as themselves.

Everyone can improve the image of women in the work place by refusing to allow women's contributions to be discounted. Women's ideas and statements are too often interrupted or ignored during group discussions. We can stop this behavior by insisting on hearing a speaker out. Often a simple statement like "I don't think we heard all of Alice's thoughts. I'd like to know what else she had to say," or "I believe Margaret's statement a few minutes ago had merit. I'd like us to go back to it and give it some consideration" will work. We can help one another by reminding the group that an idea now being touted as "good thinking" had its origins in an overlooked statement made by a woman a few minutes ago.

We can also empower one another by cushioning criticism with encouragement. A woman's mistakes are often blown out of proportion and used as evidence that she isn't qualified to compete in the workplace. Sometimes we can be overly critical of another woman's performance out of anxiety that her behavior will reflect on all women. And probably it does! Nevertheless, we need each others' encouragement, compassion and guidance as we inevitably trip over some of the many obstacles in our path toward success.

Empowering through Providing Information

Information is power; it is impossible to succeed in a system we don't understand. Too often women lack the information that would enable us to exercise power within our organizations. This is due in part to the tendency within organizations to exclude lower level employees from knowledge of operational procedures. Kanter explains that people at the bottom of the hierarchy are denied such basic information as the salary range for certain job grades, who is in charge of what, and even the identities and positions of top officials. Women, because we lack contacts who are willing to educate us, are all the more apt to be deprived of information. Sponsors, mentors and peers are the people most likely to informally provide an aspiring woman with behind-the-scenes information about how her organization functions. In any of these roles, you can share what you know about office politics: who influences whom, who has what kind of power, and what strategies work best in dealing with particular personalities. You can tell another woman how decisions *really* get made (maybe it is said they get made at a designated meeting when they are actually made on the golf course or over lunch). As a helpful peer or experienced guide you can identify protocol, subtle norms and unspoken rules of the organization so that a woman needn't learn about them as a result of having violated them. You can point out people who are likely to be supportive allies, and alert her to people whose prejudice may present obstacles.

Other kinds of information should be provided more formally. As you gain position power you can use your influence to see that information that is unnecessarily hidden becomes available to others. You can encourage policies that guarantee access to operating data, minutes of meetings, information about budgets, salaries, perquisites and fringe benefits.

Empowering through Training

Offering employees the opportunity to participate in training programs can be a highly effective way to empower women. If you have influence you can encourage your organization to pay for women to participate in remedial programs to help them develop skills in which they may be deficient as a result of female socialization patterns. (An example is the assertiveness training module which focuses directly on influencing behavior and increasing awareness of one's power style). Such programs serve the dual purpose of building skills and promoting contacts and supportive relationships between women coworkers.

Programming training experiences for mixed groups of men and women can break down barriers to collaboration between the sexes and can also lay the groundwork for peer alliances. Particularly useful would be special seminars that promote men and women as equals and focus on understanding commonalities rather than emphasizing differences. If men and women of various levels jointly participated in training experiences, a woman would have the opportunity to be known by higher level members of her organization. Consequently, there would be an increased likelihood that managers and supervisors would introduce her to other members of the organization and possibly elect to serve as mentors and sponsors.

It would also be helpful to offer training programs solely for men to educate them on how their behavior can undermine a woman's effectiveness. Many managers are unaware of the negative impact of such traditional male behaviors as "protecting" a woman by making difficult decisions for her, giving her easy assignments, singling her out through overly polite and solicitous treatment and taking over for her in emergencies. Men in management positions can be educated about strategies that empower a woman, such as offering her challenging assignments, allowing her to make important decisions, letting others know that she has the trust of the organization and refusing to allow people to circumvent her authority. Incentive systems can be developed that reward supervisors for successfully training and promoting women.

Empowering through Support of Outside Responsibilities

American work conditions discourage the integration of workers' lives. Competition and responsibilities often demand that upwardly striving workers devote as much as sixty hours a week to their jobs. Two-week vacations are the norm, and amount to a gesture acknowledging the human need for relaxation and time with family and friends. Adequate daycare is seriously lacking (throughout the nation there are twice as many children whose parents are seeking daycare as there are slots available). Maternity benefits must be fought for and many times are not paid at all. Paternity leaves exist in name only. Men who would like to take them fear losing status, and most organizations have no provisions for paternity leave anyway.

Regardless of their ambition and drive, very few people find satisfaction in these conditions. When male executives were asked in a recent Harris Poll what major changes they would hope to see by the year 2000, as many as 80 percent indicated they would most like to have more flexible working schedules and more time with their children.

Because society assigns primary responsibility for home and family to women, full-time working women suffer most. They juggle what amounts to *two* full-time jobs. The difficulty women face in negotiating the demands of career and motherhood is forcing many of us into either-or decisions. Kane, Parsons, and Associates recently published the results of a poll indicating that 70 percent of women executives do not have children, and 63 percent reported sacrificing their marriages, friendships, and leisure time for careers. Women not willing to forego marriage and family are turning to part-time work and less ambitious career goals — often reluctantly.

If women are to be empowered to contribute in the work place to the fullest of our desires and ability, we will need support in our outside responsibilities. The following are some suggested programs and policies you may be able to influence your organization to adopt:

- Paid maternity and paternity leaves
- On-site child care facilities
- The purchasing of slots in community daycare facilities
- Childcare assistance programs for employees earning low incomes
- Flexible working hours
- Job-sharing arrangements
- An increased number of part-time positions
- Cafeteria-style benefits, whereby employees may select those best suited to their needs from a number of benefits

Empowering through Modifying the Structure of Organizations

Organizational structure plays a critical role in shaping a woman's success. The hierarchical pyramid continues to leave the vast majority of women at the lower levels, facing overwhelming obstacles to advancement. The empowerment of women in the work place requires organizational reform, and such changes come slowly. Your attempts to influence reform will call for a thorough understanding of your organization, as well as much persuasiveness and persistence.

Kanter advocates structural changes that will increase autonomy and opportunities to exercise authority at lower levels of an organization. For example, "flattening the hierarchy" by removing some of the levels of authority would reduce the likelihood of people being overmanaged and increase opportunities for exercising discretion, taking on nonroutine responsibilities and gaining greater visibility.

People at lower levels could be empowered through the creation of more project teams or task groups. Members of a team are empowered by seeing a project through from beginning to end, with total control over the process. They are given decision-making rights and increased professional responsibilities that allow them to use their skills and explore their potential.

Powell maintains that structural changes are needed to remedy the problem of women who get stuck in *velvet ghettos* — those jobs and positions thought to be the natural province of women. For example, positions in personnel, public relations, consumer affairs and corporate social responsibility are seen as requiring empathy, high social sensitivity, and well-developed interpersonal skills, traits stereotyped as feminine. These positions tend to be staff functions, considered less important than line functions like sales, finance and production. People assigned to staff functions have less power and are less likely to be promoted to positions requiring leadership, forcefulness, independence and ambition. (It appears that some organizations choose to place women in velvet ghettos in hopes of meeting the demands of women's growing career aspirations, as well as the requirements of affirmative action policies, without upsetting the preexisting balance of power.)

Powell describes two needed modifications:

1. The upgrading of the status of velvet-ghetto functions, with a recognition that such functions contribute greatly to the productivity of line functions and also provide organizations with a way to exercise social responsibility.

2. The institution of bridges by which a woman can move from a staff track to a line track, avoiding a career track defined by stereotypes. Secretaries, whose jobs also tend to be dead ends, could be groomed for future positions of advanced responsibility, thereby making it possible for them to get on a management track.

As women in today's work force, we cannot afford to support the conventional concept that power is too limited to share. If we do, we will continue to find ourselves excluded from those who wield power and influence. We must see to it that opportunities are offered and obstacles removed to enable women, now and in the future, to contribute to their fullest.

Empowering one another is our responsibility to society; only through the appreciation and integration of female values, qualities, and skills will the American work place become a fully productive and fully human environment. Empowering one another is also our responsibility to ourselves; none of us operates in isolation. We owe a debt of trust to those women who struggled for equality before us and to those who will come after.

Bibliography

Introduction

Bennis, Warren. "False Grit." *Savvy,* June 1980.

Bunker, Barbara B., and Edith W. Seashore. "Power, Collusion, Intimacy-Sexuality, Support: Breaking the Sex-Role Stereotypes in Social and Organizational Settings." In Carney, C. G., and S. L. McMahon (eds.) *Exploring Contemporary Male/Female Roles.* San Diego: University Associates, Inc., 1977.

French, J.R.P., and B. Raven. "The Bases of Social Power." In D. Cartwright (ed.) *Studies of Social Power.* Ann Arbor, Michigan: Institute for Social Research, 1959.

Miller, Jean B. *Toward a New Psychology of Women.* Boston: Beacon Press, 1977.

Chapter 1. Personal Power

Blanchard, Kenneth. *The One-Minute Manager.* San Diego: Blanchard-Johnson Publishing Co., 1981.

Friere, P. *Pedagogy of the Oppressed.* New York: The Seabury Press, 1970.

Gallwey, Timothy W. *The Inner Game of Tennis.* New York: Random House, 1973.

Harragan, Betty L. *Games Mother Never Taught You: Corporate Gamesmanship for Women.* New York: Warner Books, 1978.

Kanter, Rosabeth Moss. *Men and Women of the Corporation.* New York: Basic Books, Inc., 1977.

McClelland, David C. "The Importance of Learning in the Formation of Motives." In Atkinson, J. W. (ed.) *Motives in Fantasy, Action and Society.* Princeton, New Jersey: Van Nostrand, 1959.

Thurman, Judith. "Power: The Hang-Ups, the Drives, the Price, the Joys." *Ms.* magazine, December 1982.

Chapter 2. Sex-Role Stereotypes

Bem, Sandra Lipsitz. "Androgyny Vs. the Tight Little Lives of Fluffy Women and Chesty Men." *Psychology Today.* September 1975.

Fasteau, Marc F. *The Male Machine.* New York: McGraw-Hill Book Co., 1974.

Goldfarb, Muriel, and Mara Gleckel. *Ego Images and Success Workbook.* MG Women's Counseling Service, 61 East 77 St., New York, NY 10021.

Greenburg, Selma. *Right From the Start: A Nonsexist Approach to Child Rearing.* Boston: Houghton Mifflin Co., 1978.

Hammer, Signe. "When Women Have Power Over Other Women." *Ms.* magazine, September 1978.

Kanter Rosabeth Moss. *A Tale of "O"; On Being Different.* New York, Harper and Row, 1980. Videotape from Goodmeasure, Inc., P.O. Box 3004, Cambridge, MA 02139.
—— *A Tale of "O"; On Being Different.* New York, Harper and Row, 1980 and videotape from Goodmeasure, Inc., P.O. Box 3004, Cambridge, MA 02139.

Lindgren, Astrid Ericsson. *Pipi Longstocking.* New York: Viking Press, 1950.

Chapter 3. Risk Taking

Abramson, P. R., J. H. Goldberg, and L. M. Abramson. "The Talking Platypus Phenomenon: Competency Ratings as a Function of Sex and Professional Status." *Psychology of Women Quarterly,* 2 (2) 114-24, 1977.

Hennig, M. and A. Jardim. *The Managerial Woman.* New York: Simon & Schuster, 1976.

Horner, Matina. "Femininity and Successful Achievement: A Basic Inconsistency." In Bardwick, J. M., E. Douvan, M. S. Horner, and D. Gutmann, *Feminine Personality and Conflict.* Belmont, California: Brooks/Cole, 1970.

Horner, Matina. "Follow-Up Studies in the Motive To Avoid Success in Women." Symposium Presentation, American Psychological Association, Miami, Florida, September, 1970.

Janda, L. H., K. E. O'Grady, and C. F. Capps. "Fear of Success in Males and Females in Sex-Linked Occupations." *Sex Roles: A Journal of Research,* 4(1): 43:50, 1978.

Josefowitz, Natasha. *Paths To Power.* Reading, Massachusetts: Addison-Wesley Publishing Co., 1980.

Rohrbaugh, Joanna Bunker. *Women: Psychology's Puzzle.* New York: Basic Books, 1979.

Tresemer, D. W. "Do Women Fear Success?" *Signs: Journal of Women in Culture and Society,* 1:863-74, 1976.

Thomas, Lewis. *The Medusa and the Snail: More Notes of a Biology Watcher.* New York: Viking Press, 1979.

Chapter 4. Women and Money

Auel, Jean M. *The Clan of the Cave Bear.* New York: Crown Publishers, 1980.

Friedan, Betty. *The Second Stage.* New York: Summit Books, 1981.

Calano, Jimmy, and Jeff Salzman. *Real World 101.* Boulder, Colorado: New View Press, 1982.

Cohen, William A. and Marshall E. Reddick. *Successful Marketing for the Small Business.* New York: American Management Association, 1981.

Gornick, Vivian and Barbara K. Moran (eds.). *Women in Sexist Society: Studies in Power and Powerlessness.* New York: Basic Books, 1971.

Hughes, Charles L. *Goal Setting: Key to Individual and Organizational Effectiveness,* New York, ANACOM, 1965.

Lawrence, Micheal. *Playboy's Investment Guide.* New York: Playboy Paperbacks, 1969.

Nelson, Paula. *The Joy of Money.* New York: Bantam Books, 1975.

Rosenberg, Tina. "Running on Empty." *Savvy*, November 1982.

Ross, Ruth. *Prospering Woman*. Mill Valley, California: Whatever Publishing, Inc., 1982.

Toffler, Alvin. *The Third Wave*. New York: William Morrow & Co., 1980.

Watt, Ian. *The Rise of the Novel: Studies in Defoe, Richardson and Fielding*. Berkeley: University of California Press, 1959.

Chapter 5. Making Presentations
Sarnoff, Dorothy. *Make the Most of Your Best: A Complete Program for Presenting Yourself and Your Ideas with Confidence and Authority*. New York: Doubleday, 1981.

Chapter 6. Criticism
La Bella, Arleen, Dolores Leach, and Rob Rutherford. *Managing Assertively Trainers Manual*. Boulder, Colorado: Rutherford Training Workshops, 1981.

Miller, Jean B. *Toward a New Psychology of Women*. Boston: Beacon Press, 1976.

Simon, Sidney B. *Negative Criticism and What to Do About It*. Niles, Illinois: Argus Communications, 1978.

Smith, Manual J. *When I Say No I Feel Guilty*. New York: Dial Press, 1975.

Chapter 7. Collaboration: The Winning Skill
Bardwick, Judith M. *The Psychology of Women: A Study of Bio-Cultural Conflicts*. New York: Harper & Row, 1971.

Connor, Daryl R. and Palmgren, Charles L. *Building Synergistic Work Teams to Cope with Organizational Change.* O. D. Resources Press, 1980. P.O. Box 95344, Atlanta, GA 30347.

Deutsch, Morton. *The Resolution of Conflict: Constructive and Destructive Processes.* New Haven, Connecticut: Yale University Press, 1973.

Fisher, Roger and William Ury. *Getting to Yes: Negotiating Agreement Without Giving In.* Boston: Houghton Mifflin Company, 1981.

Friedan, Betty. *The Second Stage.* New York: Summit Books, 1981.

Greenberg, Selma. *Right From the Start: A Non-Sexist Approach to Childrearing.* Boston: Houghton Mifflin Co., 1978.

Greenburger, Francis with Thomas Kiernan. *How to Ask for More and Get It: The Art of Creative Negotiation.* Chicago: Doubleday, 1978.

Harragan, Betty L. *Games Mother Never Taught You: Corporate Gamesmanship for Women.* New York: Warner Books, Inc., 1978.

Hennig, Margaret and Anne Jardim. *The Managerial Woman.* New York: Pocket Books, 1976.

Horner, Matina. "Fail: Bright Women," *Psychology Today,* 1969, 3 (6): 36.

Konner, Melvin. *The Tangled Wing: Biological Constraints of the Human Spirit.* New York: Holt, Rinehart & Winston, 1982.

Loughran, Elizabeth. *Collaboration in Work Settings.* Unpublished doctoral dissertation. University of Massachusetts at Amherst, 1981.

McClelland, D. C. "The Importance of Learning in the Formation of Motives." In Atkinson, J. W. (ed.) *Motives in Fantasy, Action and Society.* Princeton, New Jersey: Van Nostrand, 1958.

Mill, Cyril R. and Lawrence C. Porter. "How to Choose Between Strategies of Conflict and Collaboration." In *Reading Book for Laboratories in Human Relations Training.* Washington, D.C.: NTL Institute.

Sargent, Alice G. *Training for Androgyny.* NTL Reader Supplement Book, Amherst, MA., 1976.

Schaef, Anne Wilson. *Women's Reality: An Emerging Female System in the White Male Society.* Minneapolis: Winston Press, 1981.

Chapter 8. Personal/Professional Balance

Adams, John D. *Understanding and Managing Stress.* San Diego: University Associates, 1980.

Friedan, Betty. *The Second Stage.* New York: Summit Books, 1981.

Josefowitz, Natasha. *Paths to Power.* Reading, Massachusetts: Addison-Wesley, 1980.

Seashore, C. and E. W. Seashore. "Managing Stress by Building Support Systems." In R. A. Luke (ed.) *The Dallas Connection.* Washington, D.C.: National Training and Development Service, 1974.

Chapter 9. Empowering One Another

Bayes, M. and P. Newton. "Women in Authority. A Social-Psychological Analysis." *Journal of Applied Behaviorial Sciences*, vol. 14, No. 1, 1978.

Friere, P. *Pedagogy of the Oppressed*. New York: The Seabury Press, 1970.

Galligan, P. and Stephanie Riger."Women in Management. An Exploration of Competing Paradigms." *American Psychologist*, 1980, 35.

Hennig, M. and A. Jardim. *The Managerial Woman*. Pocket Books, 1977.

Josefowitz, Natasha. *Paths to Power*. Reading, Massachusetts: Addison-Wesley Publishing Company, 1980.

Kanter, Rosabeth Moss. *Men and Women of the Corporation*. New York: Basic Books, 1977.

Larwood, L., and J. Blackmore. "Sex Discrimination in Managerial Selection: Testing Predictions of the Vertical Dyad Linkage Model." *Sex Roles*, 4, 1978.

McClelland, D. and D. Burnham. "Power Is the Great Motivator." *Harvard Business Review*, 1976.

Powell, Gary N. "Career Development and the Woman Manager—A Social Power Perspective." *Personnel*, 1980, 57.

Shapiro, E. C., F. P. Haseltine, and M. P. Rowe. "Moving Up: Role Models, Mentors, and the Patron System." *Sloan Management Review*, Vol. 19, No. 3, Spring 1973.

Staines, G. Tazis and T. E. Jayaratne. "The Queen Bee Syndrome." *Psychology Today*, January 1974.

Thurman, Judith. "Power: the Hang Ups, the Drives, the Price, the Joys." *Ms*, December 1982.

Tilley, A. C. *Interpersonal Conflict Resolution.* Glenview, Illinois: Scott, Foresman and Company, 1975.

Van Wagner, K. and C. Swanson. "From Machiavelli to Ms: Differences in the Male-Female Power Styles." *Public Administration Review*, 39, 1979.

SOMERSET COUNTY COLLEGE

LIBRARY

North Branch, New Jersey